AF600148

THE CATHOLIC UNIVERSITY OF AMERICA
CANON LAW STUDIES
No. 103

THE CLERICAL OBLIGATIONS OF CANONS 139 AND 142

AN HISTORICAL SYNOPSIS AND COMMENTARY

A DISSERTATION

Submitted to the Faculty of Canon Law of the Catholic University of America in Partial Fulfillment of the Requirements for the Degree of

DOCTOR OF CANON LAW

BY

JOSEPH BERNARD BRUNINI, A.B., S.T.B., J.C.L.
Priest of the Diocese of Natchez

THE CATHOLIC UNIVERSITY OF AMERICA
WASHINGTON, D. C.
1937

Nihil Obstat:

VALENTINUS T. SCHAAF, O.F.M., J.C.D.

Censor Deputatus.

Washingtonii, D. C., die XIV Maii, 1937.

Imprimatur:

✠ RICHARDUS O. GEROW, D.D.,

Episcopus Natchetensis.

Natchez, die XVIII Maii, 1937.

Printed by

THE PAULIST PRESS

New York, N. Y.

TO MY MOTHER AND FATHER

TABLE OF CONTENTS

PAGE

CHAPTER IX

FOREWORD

TITLE Three of the Second Book of the Code of Canon Law is concerned with the obligations of clerics. The title embraces only twenty canons and these may be divided into canons concerning positive obligations and those treating of negative obligations, having in mind, of course, that the distinction is not always clear-cut. Most of the positive obligations are treated in the Code before the negative ones. Among negative obligations are: (1) Those arising from chastity. (2) The offering of security, going bond, *fideiussio.* (3) Activities which are not becoming to the clerical state. (4) Activities which, while not absolutely unbecoming, are nevertheless foreign to the clerical state. (5) The prohibition of leaving the diocese for a notable length of time.

This dissertation treats of those negative obligations contained in Canons 139 and 142. Canon 139, after the general prohibition in the first paragraph against such things as are foreign to the clerical state, determines in three separate paragraphs certain specific occupations which are included in this prohibition. The prohibited occupations are medicine and surgery, the holding of public office, the office of notary public, the administration of lay property, the office of advocate and procurator, the participation in civil criminal trials, and the soliciting and accepting of legislative positions. Canon 142 is directed against clerics entering upon business undertakings of a commercial nature. As these two canons present little new legislation their historical development is highly important for their present interpretation.

As a basis for the prohibitions of Canons 139 and 142 the legislators throughout the history of the Church have evoked the saying of St. Paul in 2 Timothy ii. 4: "No man being a soldier to God entangleth himself with secular businesses." Laws on this subject are found in the Apostolic Canons,[1] and in such early councils as Carthage, Elvira and Chalcedon. All the Christian emperors whose laws are found in the Theodosian Code—from Constantine to Val-

[1] Canons 6, 81, 83.

entinian—granted many immunities to clerics and in general enforced the details of ecclesiastical legislation. Such provisions are also found in the Novels of Justinian. The details of this civil and ecclesiastical legislation are reserved to the treatment of the specific provisions in the Code, as examined separately in the various chapters.

Considered from the viewpoint of immunity from obligations foreign to the clerical state, the Code provides in Canon 121 that no one should force a cleric into such occupations. The question of immunity, however, is not here treated *ex professo.*

The writer takes this occasion to express his gratitude to His Excellency, the Most Reverend Richard Oliver Gerow, D.D., Bishop of Natchez, for the opportunity afforded for advanced study and for his constant encouragement. He also acknowledges his deep gratitude to the Faculty of the School of Canon Law, under whose supervision this dissertation was prepared.

CHAPTER I

INTRODUCTION

Canon 139, § 1. Ea etiam quae, licet non indecora, a clericali tamen statu aliena sunt, [clerici] vitent.

§ 2. Sine apostolico indulto medicinam vel chirurgiam ne exerceant; tabelliones seu publicos notarios, nisi in Curia ecclesiastica, ne agant; officia publica, quae exercitium laicalis iurisdictionis vel administrationis secumferunt, ne assumant.

§ 3. Sine licentia sui Ordinarii ne ineant gestiones bonorum ad laicos pertinentium aut officia saecularia quae secumferant onus reddendarum rationum; procuratoris aut advocati munus ne exerceant, nisi in tribunali ecclesiastico, aut in civili quando agitur de causa propria aut suae ecclesiae; in laicali iudicio criminali, gravem personalem poenam prosequente, nullam partem habeant, ne testimonium quidem sine necessitate ferentes.

§ 4. Senatorum aut oratorum legibus ferendis, quos *deputatos* vocant, munus ne sollicitent neve acceptent sine licentia Sanctae Sedis in locis ubi pontificia prohibitio intercesserit; idem ne attentent aliis in locis sine licentia tum sui Ordinarii, tum Ordinarii loci in quo electio facienda est.

Canon 142. Prohibentur clerici per se vel per alios negotiationem aut mercaturam exercere sive in propriam sive in aliorum utilitatem.

The first paragraph of Canon 139 declares that clerics must avoid those pursuits which, granted that they are not unbecoming, are nevertheless foreign, to the clerical state. The following three paragraphs of this canon mention various occupations which are included in this general prohibition of paragraph one. There is no conclusive argument to demonstrate that the last three paragraphs enumerate all of the occupations which might be termed *foreign* to the clerical state. Had the codifiers considered them as containing such an exclusive enumeration it seems that paragraphs two, three and four would have been listed as subdivisions of paragraph one and not as separate paragraphs. Granted that the list is not fully comprehensive the ordinary would have the power to list other occupations under the general prohibition of paragraph one. Maroto, for example, states that the ordinary and provincial councils could bring certain political activities under this general prohibition.[1] Several authors maintain that some transactions which do not fall strictly under the forbidden trading of Canon 142 are forbidden by virtue of the general provisions of Canon 139, § 1.[2]

In recent concordats the governments of a number of States have provided for the exemption of clerics from the occupations prohibited by Canon 139. In several of the concordats clerics and religious have been expressly declared exempt from jury duty and from service on so-called "People's Tribunals," and from other duties which "according to Canon Law are incompatible with the clerical or religious state." [3]

Those Subject to These Prohibitions

All clerics are subject to the prohibitions of Canons 139 and 142. Canon 108, § 1, defines a cleric as one who has received the first clerical tonsure. Canon 592 subjects all religious to the obligations binding on clerics by virtue of Canons 139 and 142. The Code defines

[1] Maroto, *Institutiones*, I, n. 566, nota 5.

[2] *Cf.* below, p. 79.

[3] Concordat with Latvia, November 3, 1922, Art. IX—*AAS*, XIV (1922), 577-581; Concordat with Bavaria, January 24, 1925, Art. I, II—*AAS*, XVII (1925), 41-56; Concordat with Poland, June 2, 1925, Art. V—*AAS*, XVII (1925), 273-287; Concordat with Lithuania, December 10, 1927, Art. V—*AAS*, XIX (1927), 425-434; Concordat with Italy, June 7, 1929, Art. IV, V—*AAS*, XXI (1929), 275-295; Concordat with Austria, May 1, 1934, Art. XIX, XXII—*AAS*, XXVI (1934), 249-283; Concordat with Germany, September 10, 1933, Art. I, VI, VII, XXXIII—*AAS*, XXV (1933), 389-414. Similar provisions are found in the concordat with the Republic of Colombia, July 5, 1888, Art. VII—*ASS*, XXI (1888), 7-12.

a religious as one who has taken the vows—public vows, of course, but not necessarily perpetual—of obedience, chastity, and poverty in an approved religious society, whether the society be lay or clerical, for men or for women.[4]

Members of societies, either of men or of women, who live a common life in imitation of religious under the government of a superior and according to approved constitutions, but without public vows of obedience, chastity, and poverty, are not religious in the strict sense of the Code.[5] Such men and women are, however, bound to the obligations of Canons 139 and 142 by virtue of Canon 679, § 1.

These societies may be either lay or clerical according to Canon 673, § 2. An example of such a clerical society is the Oratory of St. Philip Neri. The *Maestre Pie Venerine* and the *Maestre Pie Filippini* are examples of such lay societies.

Whenever the term "cleric" is used in the following pages it is understood to include, unless the context shows otherwise, not only those who have received tonsure but also all religious as well as the members of such societies as live in imitation of religious as defined in Canon 673.

Seminarians before receiving first tonsure, postulants and novices are not subject to these obligations. The propriety of their observing them while on a legitimate leave of absence is a matter for the judgment of proper authorities rather than a canonical question.[6]

To be a religious, according to the present law of the Code as established in Canon 487, it suffices that at least temporary vows in some religious society be pronounced. However, the religious state requires that stability which is effected by at least the ability to renew temporary vows.[7] Those societies, therefore, which provide for vows so absolutely temporary that they are not allowed to be renewed for life, lack the essential stability of religious societies and hence their

[4] *Cf.* Canon 488, 1° and 7°, and Canon 487.

[5] *Cf.* Canon 673, § 1.

[6] But see below, pp. 4-7, as regards the simple impediment to orders and to the licit admission to the novitiate of those who have engaged in these pursuits.

[7] Canon 488, 1°.

members are not religious in the strict sense of the Code, nor are they held to these obligations. Schäfer and Fanfani speak of such societies but offer no examples.[8]

Some religious orders—for example, the Benedictines—have members known as oblates who do not make profession. Such oblates are not truly religious and, consequently, are exempt from these obligations, provided, of course, that they have not received clerical tonsure.[9]

Third Orders Secular described in Canon 702, § 1, do not pertain to the religious state and hence are not held to these restrictions.

Military orders, taking only a vow of conjugal chastity, are not religious in the strict sense of the term. However, both the order of St. John of Jerusalem and the Teutonic Order take the three vows including that of perfect chastity in an approved religious society. They are, therefore, subject to these prohibitions.[10]

Simple Impediment to Orders

By virtue of Canon 987, 3°, a simple impediment to orders arises for those who exercise an office or administration forbidden to clerics and of which they must render an account, and obtains in force until freedom from the impediment is reëstablished by the rendering of an account and the giving up of said office or administration. This impediment would seem to arise from all of the occupations forbidden by Canons 139 and 142. Vermeersch-Creusen, however, in treating of Canon 987, 3°, refer the reader only to § 3 of Canon 139.[11] It is important to decide this point because, if a simple impediment arises from all the occupations of Canons 139 and 142, then orders cannot be conferred licitly upon those engaged in these occupations, nor can such persons exercise licitly the orders already received.[12]

8 Schäfer, *De Religiosis,* p. 30; Fanfani, *De Iure Religiosorum,* pp. 4-5.

9 Schäfer, *De Religiosis,* § 33; [Bachofen], Charles Augustine, *A Commentary on the New Code of Canon Law,* 4th ed., Vol. II, St. Louis: B. Herder, 1923, p. 90.

10 Schäfer, *De Religiosis,* § 32; Wernz, *Ius Decretalium,* III, n. 591.

11 Vermeersch-Creusen, *Epitome,* II, n. 259.

12 Canon 968.

The sources, besides mentioning such specific offices as those of procurators, plaintiffs *(actores)*, executors or tutors of minors, state also that this impediment arises in general from all curial, military and civil offices connected with public affairs of any kind[13]

Similar statements are found in Reiffenstuel, Schmalzgrueber, Gasparri, Cappello, Aertnys-Damen.[14]

It is helpful to mention here the reasons for the establishment of this impediment. They may be summed up as follows: (1) Rarely can a man be found who can fulfill one office perfectly, much less two or more offices well. (2) It is easier to follow the tendency of fulfilling temporal duties rather those of a spiritual nature. (3) Such offices endanger the liberty and discipline of the Church, making clerics dependent on civil power and temporal masters with a resultant lack of prompt obedience to ecclesiastical superiors. (4) There is danger of such men receiving sacred orders, not for the love of God, but to avoid rendering an account of their deeds. (5) This last would lead to grave inconvenience for creditors and for those to whom the account must be rendered. (6) The good name of the Church would also be endangered.

Regarding senators and deputies, Gasparri states that such are not to be forbidden the reception of orders, but the context clearly shows that he bases this on the fact that the pre-Code law for the universal Church did not prohibit these offices to clerics as such.[15] With the advent of the Code, however, since the same reasons apply, it is probable that a similar impediment arises from these occupations.

Those clerics who in contravention of Canon 142 engage in business pursuits either through themselves or others are similarly subject to this impediment, until they have given up such a pursuit and rendered an account. Gasparri held this opinion before the Code.[16]

A special consideration must be given to the professions of medi-

[13] C. 1, D. LIII; C. 1, D. LV; c. un., X, *de obligatis ad ratiocinia ordinandis vel non*, I, 19.

[14] Reiffenstuel, lib. I, tit. 19, nn. 1-7; Schmalzgrueber lib. I, tit. 19, n. 2; Gasparri, *De Sacra Ordinatione*, I, n. 553; Cappello, *De Sacra Ordinatione*, n. 521; Aertnys-Damen, *Theologia-Moralis*, II, n. 607.

[15] Gasparri, *De Sacra Ordinatione*, I, n. 552.

[16] Gasparri, *De Sacra Ordinatione*, I, n. 553.

cine and surgery. Canon 985, 6°, establishes an irregularity for clerics exercising these arts if death follows therefrom. The irregularity would similarly arise if death is notably accelerated. Before the Code, if these prohibited arts had been exercised and if it were not known that death had possibly resulted or had been notably accelerated, a dispensation *ad cautelam* was granted from the irregularity.[17] Such a procedure is likewise advisable at present.

Clerics, therefore, who exercise, without proper permission, any of the prohibited occupations of Canons 139 and 142, cannot licitly exercise the orders they have received, and until they have given up such occupations and rendered an account they cannot be promoted to higher orders.

Not only must the occupation itself be given up, but an account must also be rendered before further orders may be received. An exception may be admitted in a case wherein, after giving up the occupation, all debts have been sufficiently provided for and in the judgment of the ordinary there is danger neither of a criminal nor civil suit in which the Church could suffer a loss or be defamed.

If a cleric, after exercising a forbidden office, is ordained over the protests of a creditor, then the assets of the cleric are to be applied to his debts. If all of his debts are not covered in this way some other means must be provided. The bishop himself would be responsible if he knowingly ordained such a cleric. If the cleric has deceived the bishop, the latter can, of course, invoke a proper punishment.

Occupations That Bar Admission to the Novitiate

Canon 542, 2°, makes illicit the admission to the novitiate of those who are burdened with debts they cannot meet, or of those who are obliged to render an account or are engaged in other secular pursuits from which the religious society has reason to fear litigations or other annoyances.

Canon 677 extends these same regulations to the members of those societies of men or women living a common life in imitation of religious, but without vows.

[17] Gasparri, *De Sacra Ordinatione,* I, n. 445.

Once a dispensation has been obtained from the irregularity resulting from the illicit practice of medicine or surgery with the subsequent death of the patient, or from the simple impediments arising from the illicit practice of the other occupations of Canons 139 and 142, the one dispensed is still eligible for all non-consistorial benefices, but he cannot be named a cardinal, a bishop, an abbot or prelate *nullius,* nor a major superior in an exempt clerical society.[18]

Those Empowered to Dispense

The exercise of medicine or surgery, the serving as a public notary outside of an ecclesiastical court, the holding of public offices involving the exercise of lay jurisdiction or administration, are allowed only by reason of an apostolic indult. In those states where a pontifical prohibition against clerics holding the office of a senator or deputy has been determined recourse must likewise be had to the Holy See.

In cases involving missionaries application should be made to the Sacred Congregation for the Propagation of the Faith.[19] Otherwise the Sacred Congregation of the Council is competent for secular clerics and the Sacred Congregation for Religious for members of religious societies.[20]

Where the Code requires the permission of the ordinary, the bishop and the superior with powers of the ordinary are competent for the granting of a dispensation. Where circumstances arise peculiar to the various occupations of these two canons regarding dispensations, a special treatment will be given in the proper place.

[18] Canon 991, § 3.
[19] *Cf.* Canon 252.
[20] Canons 250 and 251.

CHAPTER II

MEDICINE AND SURGERY

Canon 139, § 2. Sine apostolico indulto medicinam vel chirurgiam [clerici] ne exerceant.

THE first specific occupation mentioned in Canon 139 as foreign to the clerical state is the practice of medicine and surgery. Surgery was first known as *medicina cum incisione et adustione,* the latter term referring to the cauterization of a wound with a hot iron as was customary in the Middle Ages.[1]

HISTORICAL CONSPECTUS

It appears that in the early days of the Church priests did actually practise medicine. St. Luke, according to most authorities, practised medicine even after being ordained, and other cases, including some which involve bishops, are also cited.[2]

The first condemnation of the custom of monks and canons regular who left their monasteries to study medicine—the study of civil law was likewise included—is found in Canon 5 of the Council of Clermont under Innocent II in the year 1130.[3] Bishops, abbots and priors not correcting this abuse were to be deprived of their own honors.

This prohibition was repeated almost verbatim in Canon 6 of the Council of Rheims, 1131,[4] and in Canon 9 of the Second Council of the Lateran, 1139.[5] The Council of Tours, 1163, in Canon 8 repeats the prohibition and provides that, if the one violating the precept fails to return within two months, he was to be avoided by all as excommunicated; and if he should then return, he must take the last

[1] C. 19, X, *de homicidio voluntario vel casuali,* V, 12.

[2] Benedict, XIV, *De Synodo Dioecesana,* XIII, 10, 5.

[3] Mansi, XXI, 438, 439.

[4] Mansi, XXI, 459.

[5] Mansi, XXI, 528.

place in the choir, in the chapter, in the refectory, etc., and only through the mercy of the Holy See can he have hope of promotion.[6] This last provision was repeated in the Third Council of the Lateran, 1179.[7]

Honorius III, 1219, extended the prohibition to the secular clergy, with the exception of certain classes, and imposed an excommunication which was to be incurred *ipso facto* and which, when incurred, was to be publicly announced.[8]

The first mention of surgery is found under Innocent III in the year 1212. A religious had performed a surgical operation in treating a tumor on the throat of a woman; afterwards the patient, not heeding his warning, exposed the tumor to the air and died. The religious was declared irregular even though he was skilled and diligent and had acted purely out of charity. The response declared that he was made irregular because death had actually followed. The response further declared that he had offended gravely in usurping a foreign office. However, because the patient had suffered death through her own neglect the religious priest should be allowed to celebrate Mass after due satisfaction.[9]

Boniface VIII freed secular clerics who had not received priesthood and those who were not pastors in the strict sense of the term from the laws of Honorius III and Clement IV.[10] However, he placed an excommunication *ipso facto* upon professed religious who, without proper permission, left their monasteries for the purpose of study, and also imposed a similar penalty upon teachers who knowingly gave instructions in law and medicine to such religious.[11]

A dispensation granted by the Sacred Congregation for the Propagation of the Faith, under date of the 4th of August, 1628, is of interest. A priest-alumnus of the English College at Douay, ready to take up his duties in persecuted England, requested a dispensa-

[6] Mansi, XXI, 1179.

[7] C. 2—Mansi, XXII, 373.

[8] C. 10, X, *ne clerici vel monachi saecularibus negotiis se immisceant*, III, 50.

[9] C. 19, X, *de homicidio voluntario vel casuali*, V, 12.

[10] C. 1, *ne clerici vel monachi saecularibus se immisceant*, III, 24, in VI°.

[11] C. 2, *ne clerici vel monachi saecularibus negotiis se immisceant*, III, 24, in VI°.

tion to practise medicine, stating that previous to his seminary studies he had done so, and that under this guise he could the more easily administer the sacraments to English Catholics, and perhaps bring heretics, especially those in danger of death, back to the faith. The Sacred Congregation requested of the Holy Father that the petition be granted with the condition that the practice of medicine be only a means and not the principal scope of the petitioner's ministry. The solicitude of Pope Urban VIII is shown by the following two conditions which he attached in granting the dispensation: the petitioner must offer his help gratis, and if his patients freely give him a remuneration he must accept nothing beyond what is necessary for his sustenance.[12]

The Third Plenary Council of Baltimore forbade to clerics the exercise of medicine and surgery both for the sake of gain and for charity.[13]

Discipline of the Code

The Code forbids to clerics the *exercise* of medicine and surgery. No mention is made of the study of these two professions and therefore it is not forbidden under the present legislation.[14] However, clerics are not allowed to attend secular or state universities without the permission of their ordinary, which is not to be granted except in case of necessity or utility for the diocese or religious society in the education of youth. Even in such cases permission should be granted only to those clerics who have received priesthood, and who give indications of upholding the honor of the sacerdotal state scholastically and morally.[15]

The word *excerere* clearly implies something done habitually. So a cleric practising these arts only in passing would not, properly speaking, be exercising these arts. The authors make no attempt to determine the precise number of times required to constitute a violation of this prohibition. It would seem that two or three times would be sufficient in serious cases involving danger of death. In other cases a more frequent repetition of acts would be necessary.

[12] S. C. de Prop. Fide, 4 aug., 1628—*Fontes*, n. 4439.

[13] *Concilii Plenarii Baltimorensis III, Acta et Decreta*, n. 82.

[14] Canon 6, 6°.

[15] S. C. Consist., dec., 30 apr., 1918—*AAS*, X (1918), 237.

However, Canon 985, 6°, makes a cleric irregular *ex delicto* if, in exercising the art of medicine or surgery forbidden to him, death follows. The cleric would incur this irregularity, even though such a case should be his first offense. This was true in the law before the Code and, since the Code introduces no new provisions in this regard, the law must receive the same interpetation now as before.[16] A religious was declared irregular because death followed on his illicit treatment of a patient, even though he was skilled and diligent and had acted purely out of charity, and the patient had died through her own neglect. In other words, there is no discussion of the number of times the religious had ignored the prohibitions to exercise these arts, and there were no reasons for the irregularity other than that death had followed from a single violation of the law.[17] Benedict XIV speaks of the law as forbidding the *exercise* of medicine and surgery and cites the above case which is based only on one offense, thereby indicating that in the case of ensuing death the question of the number of offenses does not affect the irregularity.[18] If the delict does not arise from the *exercise* of medicine or surgery, it can be said to arise from the general prohibition of Canon 139, § 1, against actions foreign to the clerical state.

There can be no doubt that all forms of surgery come under the prohibition of this canon. However, some dispute has arisen among authors as to whether or not all forms of medicine are forbidden. They mention specifically homoeopathy and the practices of the so-called "Kneipp doctors" and other naturopaths. Homoeopathy is defined as the treatment of disease by drugs, usually in minute doses, that in healthy persons would produce symptoms like those of the disease. Ayrinhac, Maroto, A Coronata, say that homoeopathy is not included in this prohibition.[19] Aichner claims that homoeopathy is included in the prohibition.[20] Ayrinhac states that it may be for-

[16] Canon 6, 3°.

[17] C. 19, X, *de homicidio voluntario vel casuali,* V, 12.

[18] Benedict XIV, *De Synodo Dioecesana,* XIII, 10, 2; 5; 7; 8; 11.

[19] Ayrinhac, *General Legislation,* p. 303; Maroto, *Institutiones,* I, n. 567; A Coronata, *Institutiones,* I, n. 201. A Coronata, however, identifies homoeopathy with the methods of the Kneipp doctors, an identification without foundation.

[20] Aichner, *Compendium Iuris Ecclesiastici,* § 73, n. 1.

bidden by particular statute and Aichner quotes such a particular statute.[21]

The theory of the Kneipp doctors, the practice of which is sometimes called naturopathy, holds that some diseases can be cured by applications of water, by exercising under certain conditions, and by spending a good deal of time in the open air. According to Ayrinhac, A Coronata, Maroto, Vermeersch-Creusen, the exercise of such an art is not included in the term *medicine.*[22] Augustine states that without a doubt such Kneipp doctors and other naturopaths are included in this prohibition.[23] In order to determine the value of these opposing opinions it is well to consider, at this point, the reasons adduced in the sources as the basis for the prohibition of medicine.

Reasons for the Prohibition Against Medicine and Surgery

The profession of medicine is forbidden first of all because it would involve too deeply in a secular calling one who has dedicated his life to the altar. Secondly, if done for gain, an additional source of scandal would arise. A third reason frequently found in the sources is the desire to protect the virtue of chastity which might be greatly endangered in the treatment of patients of the other sex. All these reasons are found in the earliest laws on the subject.[24] A fourth reason for clerics avoiding the exercise of the medical and surgical profession without an apostolic indult is found in the fact that they become irregular *ex delicto* if death follows therefrom.[25] A fifth reason alleged by Augustine is not found in the sources and, as A Coronata points out, seems to be without foundation. Augustine says that ". . . the law is aimed at the exercise of the medical pro-

[21] Ayrinhac, *General Legislation,* p. 303.

[22] Ayrinhac, *General Legislation,* p. 303; A Coronata, *Institutiones,* I, n. 201; Maroto, *Institutiones,* I, n. 567; Vermeersch-Creusen, *Epitome,* I, n. 223.

[23] Augustine, *Commentary,* II, 89.

[24] Council of Clermont (1130), Canon 5—Mansi, XXI, 438, 439; Council of Rheims (1131), Canon 6—Mansi, XXI, 459; Second Council of the Lateran (1139), Canon 9—Mansi, XXI, 528.

[25] Canon 985, 6°.

fession as such and intended to safeguard the honor of real physicians against usurpers and bunglers." [26]

Because of the four reasons stated above it would seem that homoeopathy and naturopathy are included under this prohibition. The cleric could eliminate with little difficulty the element of profit and could take the proper precautions in regard to chastity, but he could hardly practise such involved secular arts without neglecting the duties of his calling and, even if he should be able to provide for such duties, there would always be present a grave danger of incurring the irregularity of Canon 985, 6°. Death could easily follow from the practice of homoeopathy and in the Kneipp treatments it is quite possible for the patient to contract pneumonia, for example, and so succumb to his illness. The irregularity would be incurred even though death followed through no professional fault of the cleric. Another reason for the inclusion of such practices under this prohibition is that the Code forbids medicine without any qualifications. "Where the law does not distinguish neither should we distinguish." The legislator, in drawing up the law, must have had in mind the accepted understanding of the term *medicine* as being "the art of restoring and preserving bodily health, especially by means of remedial substances and regulations of diet, etc., as opposed to surgery." A number of hospitals specializing in homoeopathic treatments have been erected in this country. So it would seem that any branch of medicine would fall under this prohibition. Dentistry, particularly surgical dentistry, is also probably prohibited.

The treatment of mental diseases which only indirectly affect the health of the body was hardly contemplated by the legislator and would not come *per se* under this prohibition. In other words, only those arts which *directly* affect the health of the *body* are accepted generally as branches of medicine.

The prescribing and the confection of pharmaceutical preparations which require scientific knowledge have evidently been considered in the past as prohibited to clerics. Ferraris speaks of the Sacred Congregation of the Council as *granting permission,* even to priests, "*. . . ut possint compositiones hyacinthi, iuleporum, et alcher-*

[26] Augustine, *Commentary,* II, 89, 90; A Coronata, *Institutiones,* I, n. 201.

mos facere, et distribuere in usum pauperum . . ."[27] Such preparations require little skill. The same interpretation would seem to hold today.

If a cleric represents himself as a qualified doctor or surgeon such deception increases the gravity of his offense, but this is not required as a formal element in the transgression of this law. The same may be said in regard to the seeking of profit. The exercise of medicine and surgery is forbidden, however, even though the cleric be skilled and approved, and even though he previously exercised these arts.

All authors agree that this canon does not forbid gratuitous advice given to the infirm in regard to the ordinary household prescriptions which require no special knowledge and in cases not involving danger. The civil law agrees with this interpretation. Blat would permit even a *minor* surgical operation occasionally in regard to a friend or servant. The opinion is not without foundation provided the cleric has sufficient skill, takes necessary precautions and only an insignificant loss of blood ensue.[28] However, in all these cases prudence must be exercised, particularly in regard to patients of the other sex, lest any basis for scandal be offered.

A person performing a caesarian operation on a woman certainly dead, in order to baptize the offspring, does not exercise surgery. However, whenever possible, a cleric must forego such an operation either because of the grave prohibitions of the civil law or certainly in view of the danger of scandal.[29]

Nursing

The care or the nursing of the sick is from its very nature different from the exercise of medicine and surgery. Clerics and religious are not, therefore, forbidden the scientific study and practice of such occupations. Many religious societies, especially of

[27] Ferraris, F. Lucius, *Bibliotheca Canonica, Iuridica, Moralis, Theologica nec non Ascetica, Polemica, Rubricistica, Historica*, Ed. novissima, 9 vols., Romae, Ex Typographia Polyglotta S. C. de Propaganda Fide, 1891, "Clericus," art. 3, n. 80.

[28] Blat, *Commentarium*, II, n. 78.

[29] *Cf.* Vermeersch-Creusen (*Epitome*, I, 223), who refer to a decree of the Holy Office, 13 dec., 1899.

women, devote their lives to such a vocation. However, in all these cases the laws of Christian modesty must be scrupulously observed, as is demanded in the approbation of such societies, and as in all other cases, so here also clerics and religious must be careful to preserve their good name.[30]

A Coronata, however, points out that religious are not to be too easily excused for assisting at operations upon patients of the other sex, even though they act *ex officio*. He states that, if such a practice is not against the letter, it is certainly against the spirit of the Code.[31] Maroto also points out that in certain circumstances the care of the sick outside the same household may be incongruous for priests.[32]

In the *normae* provided by the Sacred Congregation of Bishops and Regulars for the approbation of new institutes, issued in 1901, special cautions and safeguards are required for those religious societies that propose to engage in the care of the sick and infirm.[33] Similar provisions are found in the *normae* of the Sacred Congregation of Religious issued in 1922.[34].

In 1936 the Sacred Congregation for the Propagation of the Faith in accord with the Sacred Congregation of Religious, issued a set of rules and instructions encouraging religious institutes of women in their efforts to provide medical care for mothers and infants in missionary lands, and at the same time made provisions for the proper medical instruction of the religious and for their spiritual welfare.[35]

[30] Wernz, Franciscus Xav., et Vidal, Petrus, *Ius Canonicum ad Codicis normam exactum,* Vol. II: *De Personis,* 2 ed., Romae: Universitas Gregoriana, 1928, n. 123.

[31] A Coronata, *Institutiones,* I, n. 201, nota 1.

[32] Maroto, *Institutiones,* I, n. 567, nota 2.

[33] *Normae secundum quas S. Congr. Episcoporum et Regularium Procedere Solet in Approbandis Novis Institutis Votorum Simplicium,* § II, nn. 13, 14, 15, Romae: Typis S. C. de Prop. Fide, 1901.

[34] *Normae secundum quas S. Congregatio de Religiosis in Novis Religiosis Congregationibus Approbandis Procedere Solet,* nn. 15, 16, 17, Romae: Typis Polyglottis Vaticanis, 1922.

[35] S. C. de Prop. Fide, *Instructio Religiosis Mulierum Institutis ad Tuendam Puerorum Matrumque Vitam in Locis Missionum—Periodica,* XXV (1936), 44-47.

Dispensations

In cases of absolute necessity no dispensation is required either for the practice of medicine or surgery. The laws of charity permit and at times even demand such aid. A cleric acting under such circumstances would not be subject to an irregularity even though death did ensue through some fault of his own. He should, of course be skilled in the art and should take due precautions in treating patients of the other sex.[36]

In requesting dispensation the testimony of the ordinary as to the skill of the applicant, his moral character and the truth of other facts alleged in the petition is required.

Two reasons are advanced as grounds for a dispensation to practise medicine. First, that there be no skilled doctor in the region or not enough doctors to handle the cases. The clause *attenta penuria medicorum* sometimes found in briefs is to be taken in a relative sense. The second reason is the poverty of the cleric or of his family which can be relieved only through honest gain from the art of medicine. The cleric is not allowed to demand a fee but can accept the voluntary offerings of his patients; he must not, however, accept anything from the poor.[37]

There are no dispensations on record permitting clerics or religious to exercise surgery requiring incisions or the loss of blood. The usual formula for faculties granted to missionaries by the Sacred Congregation for the Propagation of the Faith excludes such permission. In cases of absolute necessity, however, surgery is licit without a dispensation.[38] The opening of veins and the otherwise letting of blood, *medicinae purgativae,* have been expressly forbidden.[39]

The Sacred Congregation for the Propagation of the Faith has

[36] S. C. Concilii, 9 febr., 1669—*Vic. Ap. Tungnini—Fontes,* n. 2811; S. C. de Prop. Fide—C. P. 28 nov., 1641, *Mission. Aethiopiae—Collectanea* (ed. 1893), n. 334.

[37] Benedict XIV, *De Synodo Dioecesana,* XIII, 10, 7; S. C. C., 16 febr., 1884 —*ASS,* XVI (1883-1884), 531-533; S. C. C., 8 mart., 1884—*ASS,* XVI (1883-1884), 539-543.

[38] Vermeersch-Creusen, *Epitome,* I, 533, § 44.

[39] S. C. de Prop. Fide (C. G.—Bardstown), 13 maii, 1816, ad I—*Fontes,* n. 4705; S. C. de Prop. Fide, 20 nov., 1626—*Fontes,* n. 4434.

stated that the restriction concerning cauterizations and incisions placed in the faculty to practise medicine does not forbid the use of light cauterizations and similar measures, unless such would endanger the life or the members of the patient.[40]

Dispensation was granted for five years by the Sacred Congregation of the Council to a monk to practise medicine in favor of pilgrims to a monastery where there were no lay doctors in the immediate vicinity. However, in spite of the fact that the monk had practised surgery with great skill in his own city for many years before receiving orders, he was not allowed to take up again this art.[41]

The same congregation gave the same faculty to a pastor for a period of three years. The dispensation was based on the following facts: (1) There was no lay doctor in the place because the people were unable to support one. (2) On the testimony of his archbishop the pastor was able to fulfill all of his pastoral duties. (3) The people were most grateful for his aid. (4) The money which he received was not to be compared to the salary of a doctor, but rather to a gift of gratitude. (5) The pastor needed the money for his sustenance.[42]

Penal Sanctions

Canon 2379 provides that clerics who put aside the clerical habit or who refuse to wear the tonsure in regions where it is required are to be given a severe warning. If there be no amendment within a month clerics in tonsure and minor orders, who so act without a legitimate cause, lose their status as a cleric *ipso facto*, with all the privileges of the clerical state. Clerics in major orders are presumed to have resigned any office they may possess and the office is considered vacant. Major clerics are also to be suspended from the orders already received. If such clerics should publicly take up an occupation foreign to the clerical state they are to be warned again and

[40] S. C. de Prop. Fide, 27 iun., 1701 (N. Missionarius in Africa)—*Collectanea* (ed. 1893), n. 339.

[41] S. C. C., 16 febr., 1884—*ASS,* XVI (1883-1884), 531-533.

[42] S. C. C., 8 mart., 1884—*ASS,* XVI (1883-1884), 542.

if they have not amended their ways within three months from this ultimate warning they are to be deposed.

Hence any cleric laying aside his habit and taking up the prohibited occupations of Canon 139 would be subject to these penalties. One might argue that it hardly seems necessary that the cleric lay aside his clerical garb in order to be subject to the deposition, which is to be imposed three months after the second warning, as in many instances the fact that the cleric retained, rather than gave up, his clerical garb would increase the amount of scandal given. However, since penalties are to be interpreted strictly [43] this sanction as such could hardly be applied unless the cleric actually put aside his habit. Recourse could and should be made to Canon 2222.

In addition to the above penalties the illicit exercise of medicine or surgery on the part of clerics gives rise to an irregularity *ex delicto* if death follows therefrom.[44] As pointed out on pages 10 and 11, this irregularity is incurred when death occurs even after the first offense. It is clear that the death of the patient is not intended for if it were, this irregularity would be identical with that incurred through an act of voluntary homicide.[45]

Before the Code he who even licitly gave aid incurred the irregularity, if the cause of accidental death arose from a lack of diligence. Since the Code, however, no irregularity is incurred through the death of the patient, if the cleric has been granted an apostolic indult. Canon 986 requires that the offense be a grave sin. Such sin is present if a cleric exercises these professions without the proper faculties. Ignorance of the existence of the law establishing this irregularity does not excuse a delinquent from the irregularity, but since the irregularity arises *ex delicto*, the *delictum* itself presupposes a mortal sin. Hence if the cleric labors under an ignorance which precludes mortal sin the irregularity *ex delicto* will also be precluded.[46]

A cleric who exercises the art of medicine or surgery in a case of dire necessity performs his acts licitly and therefore incurs no irregu-

[43] Canons 19 and 2219, § 1.
[44] Canon 985, 6°.
[45] Canon 985, 4°.
[46] *Cf.* Canon 988.

larity, even if the death of the patient should result therefrom. Nor would he incur the irregularity if the sick person, unskilfully treated by him in the beginning, eventually dies through the fault of a doctor afterwards entrusted with the case. Finally, under the law of the Code a cleric would not contract any irregularity if unintentional or unforeseen mutilation resulted from his illicit exercise of medicine or surgery.

CHAPTER III

THE HOLDING OF PUBLIC OFFICE

Canon 139, § 2. Sine apostolico indulto . . . officia publica, quae exercitium laicalis iurisdictionis vel administrationis secumferunt [clerici], ne assumant.

CANON 139 forbids clerics to assume a public office which involves the exercise of lay jurisdiction or administration. As pointed out on pages 2 to 4 the word cleric here includes also religious and those living a common life in imitation of religious, but without vows. A dispensation from this prohibition requires an apostolic indult. Canon 121 of the Code considers under the title of clerical rights and privileges the exemption from public civil offices and duties foreign to the clerical state.

HISTORICAL CONSPECTUS

Constantine exempted clerics from such public duties and issued a special prohibition against certain heretics who annoyed clerics by nominating them for such positions.[1] All the Christian emperors whose laws are found in the Theodosian Code passed similar exemptions.[2]

Justinian included this earlier legislation in the Code [3] and in his Novels, and mentioned some of the specific duties forbidden to all clerics and monks. They could not be receivers or collectors of taxes, recorders of public or private property, superintendents of households or attorneys to conduct litigation, nor act as sureties for any of the above-mentioned purposes. Justinian expressly stated that the reason for his legislation was the protection of religious establishments from injury, and that the holy services of the Church should suffer no interference.

As regards penalties, he enacted that if any member of the

[1] Theodosian Code, XVI, 2, 1; XVI, 2, 2; XVI, 2, 9.

[2] Theodosian Code, XVI, 2, 10; 11; 12; 14; 15; 21; 24; 29; 38; 40; 42; 45.

[3] Codex (1.3), 6.

clergy should accept any of the forbidden duties the bishop should collect a fine from him for the benefit of the Church. Laymen, appointing clerics to such duties, were deprived of the right of legal action against the church or monastery to which the cleric or monk belonged, and they were not allowed to enter suit directly against the cleric or monk. On the other hand, if the public should have suffered any loss on this account, those who had entrusted clerics with such duties would be compelled to repair the loss.[4]

During the early years of persecution Christians in general naturally avoided public offices because of the universal superstition in the Roman Republic, because frequently public duties were intimately connected with pagan worship, and because there remained danger of persecution. So during these times it was not the clergy but rather the laymen who on occasion entered too freely into such offices.[5]

The Apostolic Canons forbade bishops, priests, and deacons, under penalty of deposition or degradation, to engage in any secular administration.[6]

The Council of Sardica, 344, in Canon 8, warns the bishops of Africa that they should not frequent the imperial palace in search of secular dignities and civil administrations.[7]

During the Middle Ages because of the higher education of clerics and the esteem which they held in the eyes of the people, infractions were more numerous and the legislation consequently more frequent. However, clerics during these times were unable to avoid all public offices, especially those affecting the administration of justice, as the bishops were frequently the vassals of the king and the Church was content to avoid abuses.[8]

In 1659 the Sacred Congregation for the Propagation of the Faith issued an instruction to missionaries to avoid perseveringly all

[4] Novellae 123, 6.

[5] Hefele, *A History of the Christian Councils*, I, 489, 490.

[6] Apostolic Canons 7, 81, 83—Hefele, *A History of the Christian Councils*, I, 460 and 489, 490.

[7] Mansi, III, 25.

[8] Fourth Council of Toledo (633), c. 31—Mansi, X, 628; Third Council of the Lateran (1179), c. 12—Mansi, XXII, 225; Council of London (1268), c. 7—Mansi, XXIII, 1222-1223; *cf.* Chapter VII for prohibitions in criminal trials.

political matters and matters pertaining to civil administration. They were to avoid such offices even though their encumbency should offer well-founded hope for the wide diffusion of the Catholic faith. The congregation took great care that missionaries should not be influenced to overlook this instruction, on the advice or example offered by otherwise prudent and religious men. The vicar apostolic was instructed to make known the positive and serious prohibition to engage in such affairs. If any missionary should fall into the errors condemned by the congregation, he was to be dismissed from further missionary activity and sent back to Europe, lest by his imprudence he jeopardize seriously the interests of religion.

If civil princes should still insist on securing advice, the cleric should inform them what would be in accordance with the divine decrees and then should avoid the residences of such princes and pretend not to be adept in civil administration. Missionaries should avoid all factional and nationalistic questions. In church gatherings they should treat of religious matters only, and should avoid all appearances of an uprising when the people were gathered for religious purposes.[9]

A later instruction of the same congregation forbade pastors to hear civil cases brought to them by the parties (at times the party against whom the pastor rendered his decision would appeal to the state courts), except in cases of friendly compromise and where both the parties obliged themselves to abide exclusively by the judgment of the pastor or of another priest designated by the vicar apostolic.[10]

Law of the Code

There can be no doubt that the exercise of any and all the occupations mentioned in § 2 of Canon 139 requires an apostolic indult. Reference may be made to page 7 for the congregations competent in granting such dispensation.

Jurisdiction may be defined as the power of governing one's subjects through laws, decrees, mandates, precepts, sentences, etc.

[9] S. C. de Prop. Fide, instr. (*ad Vic. Ap. Societ. Mission. ad Exteros*), a. 1659—*Fontes*, n. 4463.

[10] S. C. de Prop. Fide., instr. (*ad Vic. Ap. Scopiae*), 26 sept., 1840, ad 8—*Fontes*, n. 4785.

By *administrative* power is understood the ordinary direction of one's subjects, that is, the common and daily carrying out of the laws, particularly in certain and obvious cases where there is no dispute or contention. It is the duty of one having administrative power to apply the law to individual actions, to constitute various offices and the other means for exercising this power, to supervise carefully the execution of the law, to direct and aid the subjects in observing the law through warnings, exhortations and the setting up of practical norms. In Church Law the powers of jurisdiction and administration are usually united in one and the same person, but in civil law they are usually given to distinct persons.

Some of the forbidden offices are, for example, those exercised by mayors, commissioners, judges, sheriffs, attorney-generals, prosecuting attorneys, governors, tax commissioners, state superintendents of schools, heads of municipal and state departments, etc. However, those offices which are merely consultative in character are not forbidden.[11] The prohibition binds whether these offices be elective or appointive. Canon 141 forbids all military offices. Clerics are not allowed either to hold the office of president, treasurer, secretary, etc., of public institutions or organizations for charitable purposes.[12]

However, it would seem that § 2 of Canon 139 is concerned with only those public duties which involve the *direct* and *immediate* exercise of jurisdiction and administration, though indirect exercise may be prohibited for other reasons. Therefore, those who exercise political administration by means of a vote are not subject to § 2. For the same reason clerics serving as deputies and senators are not included *per se* under this paragraph. As regards offices of a private nature clerics are granted greater liberty, yet so as to remain within the limits of Canon 139, § 3.[13]

[11] Wernz-Vidal, *De Personis*, n. 131. Vidal, however, adopts a stricter interpretation by saying that non-jurisdictional duties of an advisory nature in cities, states, etc., can hardly be accepted licitly without permission of the ordinary, since they are generally more or less connected with the burden of rendering an account.

[12] Maroto, *Institutiones*, I, n. 567; Cocchi, *Commentarium*, II, 134.

[13] On page 2 are found the provisions in recent concordats in reference to the holding of public office by clerics and religious.

CHAPTER IV

THE OFFICE OF NOTARY PUBLIC

Canon 139, § 2. Sine apostolico indulto . . . tabelliones seu publicos notarios, nisi in Curia ecclesiastica [clerici], ne agant.

Besides the general regulation against the holding of public office by clerics, Canon 139 expressly mentions the prohibition against the office of public notary, outside of ecclesiastical curiae. Canon 373, § 3, demonstrates that in ecclesiastical courts clerics are to be preferred to lay people for the position and, if the case be one involving a cleric in criminal matters, the notary must be a priest. In this thesis the office of notary is being considered merely in its negative aspect as being prohibited to clerics in civil matters. As pointed out on pages 2 to 4 the word cleric here includes also religious and those living a common life in imitation of religious, but without vows. For the positive aspect as outlined in Canons 372 to 374, 503, and 2013 to 2017, advising and at times requiring clerics to act as notaries in Church courts, the reader is referred to approved authors.

It would appear more logical had this prohibition been placed after the general provisions against the holding of such public offices, which involve lay jurisdiction or administration. In this thesis it is so transferred. For the immunity granted to clerics by the civil authorities from public duties in general and the Church's general legislation on the subject the reader is, therefore, referred to Chapter III.

Historical Notes

Innocent III, in 1211, forbade the office of notary to clerics in major orders and, as a sanction, established the punishment of excommunication and deprivation of benefice; a punishment of excommunication was also sanctioned against those who accepted public legal instruments from clerics acting contrary to this law.[1] Evidently minor clerics were not forbidden to hold office.

In matters of faith during the Inquisition the court was required strictly to appoint as notaries such clerics who had exercised a notarial office before entering the clerical state. Permission was granted for all clerics and religious, even those in sacred orders, to be public notaries in such cases.[2]

These two laws must be studied carefully for they prevailed as the only written law for over seven hundred years. The first law of Innocent III forbade the office of notary to clerics in major orders and since no distinction was made in the law the glossators held that the prohibition extended to ecclesiastical as well as to civil courts.[3] Most approved authors hold the same opinion.[4] So it seems that minor clerics could be notaries in both civil and ecclesiastical courts, while major clerics could serve in neither. The requirement that all notaries in the courts of the Inquisition be at least minor clerics and the *permission* for major clerics and religious also to serve in these courts is pointed out by the authors as a clear exception which serves only to strengthen their interpretation of the general rule.

Although this was the written law prevalent before the Code it seems clear that a contrary custom allowing secular priests to serve in ecclesiastical courts prevailed in the whole world.[5] Ojetti tries to explain the apparent contradiction between the written law and the universal custom by stating that the legislation in c. 8, X, *ne clerici vel monachi saecularibus negotiis se immisceant,* III, 50, forbade clerics to hold the office of public notary only if they did so for

[1] C. 8, X, *ne clerici vel monachi saecularibus negotiis se immisceant,* III, 50.

[2] C. 11, *de haereticis,* V, 2, in VI°.

[3] v. Glossa, *clericis in sacris,* in c. 8, X, *ne clerici vel monachi saecularibus negotiis se immisceant,* III, 50.

[4] Fagnanus, lib. III, tit. 50, n. 61; Schmalzgrueber, lib. III, tit. 50, n. 56; Smith, *Elements of Ecclesiastical Law,* II, n. 919; Vermeersch-Creusen, *Epitome,* I, n. 223, 2; A Coronata, *Institutiones,* I, n. 201; Wernz-Vidal, *De Personis,* II, n. 131; Ayrinhac, *General Legislation,* p. 304.

[5] Smith, *Elements of Ecclesiastical Law,* II, n. 919; Wernz, *Ius Decretalium,* II, n. 225, II; Ferraris, *Bibliotheca Prompta,* "Clericus," art. III, n. 67; Reiffenstuel, lib. III, tit. 50, n. 7; Schmalzgrueber, lib. III, tit. 50, n. 57.

the sake of pecuniary profit.[6] Since this opinion is contrary to the interpretation of the glossators and the majority of authors and fails to explain the permission for major clerics and religious to serve in the courts of the Inquisition, it can carry little weight.

It is remarkable that the written law was allowed to remain for such a long time until the universal custom contrary to the law was approved by the Code. Perhaps the express prohibition in the Code against the office of public notary in civil courts—certainly a rare occurrence in our times and one of relative unimportance—was a result of the desire to clarify the situation.

Law of the Code

The Code extends the old prohibition by forbidding even minor clerics to serve as notary publics in civil curiae.

Although the strict wording of the Code forbids clerics to act as public notaries except in ecclesiastical curiae, there are, nevertheless, good grounds for the opinion that clerics may act as public notaries in the drawing up of various civil documents in instances involving ecclesiastical persons. The civil law of various countries requires a civilly authorized notary public to witness and at times to accept the oath of parties in the drawing up and execution of deeds, deeds of trust, and similar legal papers. Private organizations—such as insurance companies—may also require affidavits to be witnessed by such public notaries. It hardly seems in accordance with the spirit of the Code that ecclesiastical persons should have to render an oath to a lay person when that necessity can be removed—as it is removed in a number of dioceses in the United States—by the simple expedient of having a cleric connected with the chancery office secure civil authority to act as a public notary in such cases. At times, too, this would relieve the diocese of a not inconsiderable expense and inconvenience.

Against this opinion one might urge that such papers would frequently find their way into the civil courts and would involve the cleric in litigations. However, such cases in which the court or attorneys for either side would question the actions of the notary

[6] *Catholic Encyclopedia*, "Courts, Ecclesiastical," IV, 450.

public are most rare. Clerics issue birth certificates and other papers of an ecclesiastical nature which sometimes enter into court proceedings, but this fact has no force in preventing this practice.

Another argument for allowing clerics to act as notaries in such cases can be deduced from the principles of the public law of the Church. Under a Catholic government with the union of Church and State the civil power would recognize the Church notary as giving ***public faith*** to the documents which he has witnessed in conformity with the laws of the Church. Such a government would not restrict the value of the notary's signature to the ecclesiastical court. For example, if a Church notary should witness an affidavit of a priest, the document would have value in the civil as well as in the ecclesiastical court.

In countries such as our own in which the civil authority will not recognize the authority of the Church notary, unless he has conformed with certain civil formalities, the Church certainly does not intend to interfere with its own work by forbidding clerics to secure likewise the power of a civil notary. Of course, the cleric would have to restrict the use of this power to documents involving ecclesiastical persons or things. In other words, he could not turn his office into a secular occupation.

For a treatment of the simple impediment arising from the illicit acting as notary public and a discussion of the penal sanctions involved the reader is referred to pages 4 to 7, and 17 to 18.

The Holy See alone can grant a dispensation in this matter. Circumstances justifying a dispensation will be found most rarely.

CHAPTER V

THE ADMINISTRATION OF LAY PROPERTY

Canon 139, § 3. Sine licentia sui Ordinarii [clerici] ne ineant gestiones bonorum ad laicos pertinentium aut officia saecularia quae secumferant onus reddendarum rationum . . .

Paragraph three of Canon 139 mentions those occupations the exercise of which requires for clerics the permission of their ordinaries. As pointed out on pages 2 to 4 the word cleric here includes also religious and those living a common life in imitation of religious, but without vows. The first prohibition enumerated in Canon 139, § 3, concerns the administration of property belonging to lay persons and the acceptance of secular offices that impose the obligation of rendering an account.

Historical Conspectus

St. Cyprian stated that grave concern was aroused among the bishops because a Christian, recently deceased, had provided in his testament that a certain priest should be the executor of his will. The seriousness of the fault is best judged from the penalty imposed: Mass was not to be offered for the deceased Christian and he was not to be prayed for publicly by the Church.[1]

In general, clerics have not been forbidden to act as guardians for widows and orphans, unable to care for themselves. The Council of Sardica, 344, Canons 8, 9, provided that bishops should not themselves approach the imperial halls in the numerous cases involving widows, orphans and injured parties, presented to them, but should act through a deacon or through some friend in the palace. If the case were to be brought to Rome it should first be submitted to the pope and, if he should consider the cause just, he would lend his aid in presenting it to the authorities.[2]

[1] *Cypriani Epistola ad Clerum et Plebem Furnitanorum*—Mansi, I, 904.
[2] Mansi, III, 25.

The Council of Chalcedon in Canon 3 condemned bishops, monks, and clerics who administered estates and patrimonies, excepting the guardianship of minors, the administration of ecclesiastical property by appointment of the bishop, the tutelage of orphans, of widows unable to care for themselves, and of any persons needing ecclesiastical charity.[3] This in general has been the law of the Church through the centuries.[4] An exception for the guardianship of relatives is also usually found in this legislation.

The next step was to prohibit to bishops and monks the tutorship of these persons, and to confine their care to other clerics. This was meant as a protection for the bishops so that they might have sufficient time to devote to their episcopal duties, while such tutorships could be turned over to the archpriest or to the archdeacon. Monks were forbidden such duties because of the incompatibility with the very nature of the monastic life.[5]

The civil law seconded the ecclesiastical in the enforcing of these decrees. Justinian made illegal the appointment of bishops and monks as guardians or curators of any person whomsoever; priests, deacons and subdeacons were allowed to accept the guardianship and curatorship of an estate, and particular mention was made of the administration of trusts belonging to relatives.[6]

Besides guardianship, other duties such as serving as superintendents of estates, as ministers of justice to princes or other seculars, and in general all lay jurisdiction was forbidden by the Third Council of the Lateran.[7]

Law of the Code

It will be noted that the permission to practise the occupations of § 3 may be granted by one's own ordinary. Therefore, exempt religious should request permission from their own superior. A

[3] Mansi, VII, 393, 394.

[4] Council of Toledo (633), c. 32—Mansi, X, 628; Council of Mayence (813), c. 6, 8—Mansi, XIV, 66, 67; c. 26, D. LXXXVI; c. 5, D. LXXXVII; c. 1, D. LXXXVIII; c. 1, 2, X, *ne clerici vel monachi saecularibus negotiis se immisceant*, III, 50.

[5] Fourth Council of Carthage (398), c. 17, 18, 20—c. 5, 6, 7, D. LXXXVIII.

[6] Novellae 123, 5.

[7] Third Council of the Lateran (1179), c. 12—Mansi, XXII, 225.

declarative statement of the Pontifical Commission for the authentic interpretation of the Code expressly demonstrates that pre-Code legislation, requiring permission of the Holy See to engage in activities forbidden to clerics by virtue of the prohibition here treated, has been abrogated by the Code which gives the power of granting permission to the proper ordinary.[8]

The prohibition is aimed at the care of goods pertaining to the *laity*. It does not affect, therefore: (1) The goods of the cleric; (2) the goods of his church or monastery or society; (3) the goods of another ecclesiastical person—including moral as well as physical persons.

The term *officia saecularia* used in this paragraph does not necessarily exclude public offices as Ayrinhac and Maroto state.[9] It is true that § 2 is concerned with public offices which involve the exercise of lay jurisdiction or administration, but there are public offices which do not fall under this category and which necessarily are secular offices requiring the burden of rendering an account. An example of this is the appointment by a president or governor of a cleric to act as arbitrator in a labor strike.

The phrase *rendering an account* applies not only to a reckoning of the goods or money involved, but may be concerned only with an account of the justice shown by the cleric in exercising such a secular office.[10] The rendering of the account may be required by the civil authorities or in order to vindicate one's name in the eyes of the people. In a democratic country the latter is likely to be of greater importance to the welfare of the Church than the former.

As previously stated, secular offices as used in this paragraph embraces also certain public offices which require the rendering of an account. Of course, all public offices which involve the exercise of lay jurisdiction or administration are included in § 2. However, it is necessary to keep these two categories distinct, because in securing an indult the Holy See alone is qualified as regards § 2, while one's own ordinary is capable concerning § 3. Cappello states clearly that *secular offices as* understood in § 3 include in general all

[8] June 3, 1918—*AAS*, X (1918), 344.

[9] Ayrinhac, *General Legislation*, p. 302; Maroto, *Institutiones*, I, n. 568.

[10] De Meester, *Compendium*, I, n. 381.

municipal duties. Necessarily he contemplates that such duties do not involve the exercise of lay jurisdiction or administration in the strict sense, for then they would be included in § 2 and the permission of the Holy See would be required.[11] Other duties specifically prohibited are those of president, moderator, secretary, and treasurer, even in enterprises for pious or charitable purposes, which would impose upon clerics the cares of administration, obligations and such risks. Although the Holy See expressed a desire that clerics encourage those organizations designed for the temporal aid of the faithful such as rural banks, coöperative associations, savings banks, etc., they were forbidden to hold major offices in these organizations.[12]

As stated in the historical introduction to this chapter, clerics are forbidden the administration of estates and patrimonies, excepting the guardianship of minors and orphans and widows unable to care for themselves and of such persons who are in need of ecclesiastical charity. Concerning guardianship a distinction is made between *tutela legitima* and *tutela testamentaria seu dativa.* The former refers to the guardianship of relatives even of the fourth degree according to Ferraris and Monacelli.[13]

In the terminology of the authors *tutela legitima* is placed in contradistinction to *tutela testamentaria seu dativa.* The latter concerns the guardianship of those not related to the cleric who has been made a guardian *nominatim* in the testament itself. Such guardianship is forbidden to clerics.[14]

Tutela legitima, according to practically all of the authors was not forbidden to clerics. However, and this is a fact overlooked by some modern authors, a cleric was required to secure permission of

[11] Cappello, *Summa Iuris Canonici,* I, n. 245.

[12] S. C. Consist., *Docente Apostolo,* 18 nov., 1910—*AAS,* II (1910), 910; *Fontes,* n. 2078. This decree required the permission of the Holy See, but its ruling has been modified by the Code in as far as the proper ordinary may now dispense: Pontifical Commission for the Authentic Interpretation of the Code, June 3, 1918—*AAS,* X (1918), 344.

[13] Ferraris, *Bibliotheca Prompta,* "clericus," art. 3, n. 84; Monacelli, Franciscus, *Formularium Legale Practicum Fori Ecclesiastici,* Vol. I, title 6, formula 4.

[14] *Cf.* Ferraris, *Bibliotheca Prompta,* "clericus," art. 3, n. 83, who quotes various decisions of the Rota and decrees of the Sacred Congregation of Bishops; *cf.* also "tutela," n. 53 and n. 54.

his superior to undertake such a care. This is the opinion stated by Ferraris, Pignatelli, and Monacelli.[15] These authors demonstrate that their opinion was in actual practise by stating that the pope, the Sacred Congregation of Bishops and Regulars, and individual bishops frequently issued permission for such guardianship, and give formulae that were customarily employed.

The only conclusion is that while the law did not forbid to clerics the guardianship of minors related through legitimate birth and of orphans and widows unable to care for themselves and the care in general of such persons as needed ecclesiastical charity, still they could not undertake such care without the permission of their superior. This is necessary in our present interpretation of Canon 139, § 3. Clearly no request need be sent to the Holy See for permission, as this can be obtained from a superior with the powers of an ordinary. But these cares cannot be undertaken on the private authority of the cleric.

As regards the United States the Plenary Councils of Baltimore leave no doubt that permission must be had for such guardianship. The legislation of the Second Plenary Council of Baltimore, 1866, while it exempts the care and guardianship of relatives, nevertheless requires the consent of the bishop for others. Since this legislation has not been abrogated by the Code and is still in effect it must be considered as the law proper to this country. The same law is found in the Third Plenary Council.[16]

The offices of trustee and of executors of wills are likewise forbidden to clerics by virtue of Canon 139, § 3. If relatives or persons needing ecclesiastical charity are concerned, the same commentary as given for the office of guardian is to be applied.

The Second Plenary Council of Baltimore condemned likewise the custom of depositing sums of money in the hands of priests with the understanding that the money must be returned at a certain time with interest. The council stated that from impru-

[15] Ferraris, *Bibliotheca Prompta*, "clericus," art. 3, n. 85 to 89; Pignatelli, *Consultationes*, Vol. V, consult. X, n. 4 et n. 11; Monacelli, *Formularium*, Vol. I, title 6, formula 4.

[16] *Concilii Plenarii Baltimorensis II Acta et Decreta*, n. 157; *Concilii Plenarii Baltimorensis III Acta et Decreta*, n. 82.

dence there might arise evil suspicions, disputes, litigations and calumnies which would result in grave offense to the faithful and would bring discredit upon the clergy. The fathers of the council provided, therefore, that in the future such deposits should not be accepted even under the pretext that such acceptance would be for the temporal good of the Church and were intended for use in aiding the poor or in similar pious works, unless the written permission of the bishop be previously granted.[17]

A practice somewhat similar to the above has arisen recently in this country among religious societies. These societies offer an "annuity plan" by which the faithful are invited to deposit money with the society on the agreement that the depositor be paid a fixed rate of interest, the principal sum to become the property of the society on the death of the donor. These plans differ somewhat as to details, but the above explanation is sufficient for the present treatise. Such a practice, since it involves the administration of lay property, requires the permission of the ordinary.

A recent letter from the Sacred Congregation of Religious forwarded by the Apostolic Delegate to religious superiors in this country under date of November 13, 1936, makes these annuity plans subject to the laws on alienation of ecclesiastical property, and says expressly that all the solemnities of Canon 534 must be observed. The letter further states that if the sums coalesce to an amount exceeding six thousand dollars a papal indult must be secured. This instruction may be taken as a norm likewise for secular clerics.

Dispensations

In granting a dispensation to act as guardian the ordinary will find sufficient reason in all those cases where the intervention of the cleric would constitute an act of ecclesiastical charity. In other cases not involving a question of charity, or where a lay guardian could be appointed, the ordinary should be more stringent in granting permission. The ordinary should bear particularly in mind that a cleric acting as guardian for a lay person does not enjoy the privileges of the ecclesiastical forum and, if any action be taken

[17] *Concilii Plenarii Baltimorensis II Acta et Decreta,* n. 159.

against his ward, the cleric will become involved in civil litigation. On the other hand there may arise a case in which a cleric is the only person fit to protect such wards and in such cases the cleric could be forced to undertake the guardianship.

In this regard, an interesting case of guardianship was recently decided by a New York court. A Catholic child was committed by the court to the custody of non-Catholic relatives, but the religious training of the child was entrusted to a priest of the diocese. Such a child is worthy of and needs ecclesiastical charity and the ordinary would be justified in granting a dispensation.

In view of past legislation bishops and regulars should not undertake the guardianship even of relatives, but should commit these cares to others. However, in the past regulars have been granted permission to undertake guardianship of their relatives, as appears from the formulae quoted by Ferraris and Pignatelli. They state that such permission was restricted by the provision that the regulars be not placed under the necessity of passing the night outside of the cloister.[18]

In granting permission to clerics and to regulars to act as guardians of relatives the sacred congregation and the bishops were accustomed to include the warning that they do nothing interdicted to ecclesiastical persons or foreign to the ecclesiastical state.[19] For instance if a tutor should be heir to a business concern engaged in trading the cleric could not assume personally its managerial duties. This by reason of Canon 142.

The concern of the Holy See in this legislation is illustrated by the fact that ordinaries must report if they have allowed any of their clerical subjects to accept an official position in such organizations as savings banks, coöperatives, rural banks, etc. If the ordinaries have done so they must state the number of clerics so engaged, whether the permission was granted by reason of the common good, or from the lack of capable laymen, or by reason

[18] Ferraris, *Bibliotheca Prompta,* "clericus," art. 3, nn. 86-89; Pignatelli, *Consultationes,* V, consult. X, n. 13

[19] Ferraris, *Bibliotheca Prompta,* "clericus," art. 3, n. 86; Monacelli, *Formularium,* Vol. I, title 6, formula 4; Pignatelli, *Consultationes,* V, consult. X, n. 12.

of the resultant help to religion. They must state whether or not such causes still persist. They must also show that honest people are interested in these organizations, and that they are guided by such principles which do not render unbecoming the participation of priests, and that they are rightly administered, so that there is no danger of clerics becoming involved in disputes. The ordinary must also explain the source of his knowledge. He must also report whether such occupations are harmful to the priest's religious life and whether they be a source of over-worry to the cleric. If this be the case, the ordinary must give details and suggest remedies.[20]

For a treatment of the punishments which result from a violation of the legislation explained in this chapter the reader is referred to pages 17 and 18 of this dissertation. A treatment of the simple impediment to orders of Canon 987, 3°, and of the impediment to the admission to the novitiate is found above on pages 4 to 7.

[20] S. C. Consist., *Formula servanda in relationibus dioecesanis conficiendis,* 4 nov., 1918. *Cf.* n. 48 of this formula—*AAS,* X (1918), 495.

CHAPTER VI

THE OFFICES OF PROCURATOR AND ADVOCATE

Canon 139, § 3. Sine licentia sui Ordinarii . . . procuratoris aut advocati munus [clerici] ne exerceant, nisi in tribunali ecclesiastico, aut in civili quando agitur de causa propria aut suae ecclesiae . . .

WITHOUT the permission of their ordinary the Code forbids clerics the exercise of the office of procurator or advocate except in ecclesiastical courts or in civil courts when their own welfare or that of the church to which they pertain is involved. As pointed out on pages 2 to 4 the word cleric here includes also religious and those living a common life in imitation of religious, but without vows. No doubt the general provisions enumerated in the preceding chapter against clerics entering into secular affairs were considered as embracing also the duties of advocate and procurator.[1]

HISTORICAL NOTES

Justinian, among other prohibitions, forbade all clerics to serve as an attorney to conduct a litigation.[2] The Emperor Leo refers to an act of the Apostles as depriving of office any bishop, priest, or other ecclesiastic who takes it upon himself to act as advocate. The emperor, with all due apologies, renews this prohibition, but limits the penalty for the first offense to excommunication and suspension for a time from all religious rights; a second offense would bring deprivation of office.[3]

A number of councils, during the twelfth century in particular, forbade both the study and the practice of civil law.[4] Earlier than

[1] Reiffenstuel, lib. I, tit. 37, n. 15.

[2] Novellae 123, 6.

[3] Constitution LXXXVI.

[4] Council of Clermont (1130), c. 5—Mansi, XXI, 438, 439; Council of Rheims (1131), c. 6—Mansi, XXI, 459; Second Council of the Lateran (1139), c. 9—Mansi, XXI, 528; Council of Tours (1163), c. 8—Mansi, XXI, 1179.

this, however, the Council of Mayence, 813, forbade clerics the exercise of the offices of advocate and procurator in the civil courts.[5] Gelasius II (1118-1119) allowed clerics to defend widows and orphans.[6]

The Third Council of the Lateran, 1179, repeated the previous legislation but made the exception which exists in the Code today, namely, that clerics could defend their own causes and those of their church; they could act also for those unable to care for themselves.[7] Innocent III, in 1206, declared that the same law held also for monks and canons regular.[8] The Council of Paris, 1213, repeated the prohibition and determined the penalty of excommunication *ferendae sententiae* against those possessing a sufficient benefice and having ecclesiastical dignity, and, nevertheless, acting as advocate.[9]

Gregory IX (1227-1241) repeated the law with the exceptions above enumerated and stated expressly that clerics could act for those related to them. The severe penalty enacted in the Council of Paris was not inflicted: a cleric acting as advocate for outsiders against the Church was to be deprived of his benefice.[10]

The Sacred Congregation of Bishops and Regulars, under date of the eighth of May, 1716, declared that ecclesiastics could, without permission of the bishop, act in the civil courts in their own causes, in those of their church, and in cases involving the poor and needy.[11]

Law of the Code

The Code forbids to clerics, without the permission of their ordinary, the office of procurator or advocate except in ecclesiastical courts or in civil courts when their own welfare or that of the church

[5] C. 14—Mansi, XIV, 69.

[6] C. 1, 2, D. LXXXVII.

[7] C. 12—Mansi, XXII, 225; *cf.* also c. 1, X, *de postulando,* I, 37.

[8] C. 2, X, *de postulando,* I, 37.

[9] C. 6—Mansi, XXII, 820, 821.

[10] C. 3, X, *de postulando,* I, 37; *cf.* etiam c. 1, 2, X, *ne clerici vel monachi saecularibus negotiis se immisceant,* III, 50, for similar decrees in the Council of Mayence and of Eugenius III; *cf.* c. 1, 2, *ne clerici vel monachi saecularibus negotiis se immisceant,* III, 24, in VI, for similar legislation by Honorius III, Clement IV, and Boniface VIII.

[11] S. C. Ep. et Reg., *Castri Maris,* 8 maii, 1716, ad I, II—*Fontes,* n. 1832.

to which they pertain is involved. As regards ecclesiastical courts all clerics are eligible for these offices provided the provisions of the Code are fulfilled.[12]

The glossators define a procurator in the following manner: *procurator dicitur qui mandato domini aliena negotia in iudicio administrat.* This form of procuratorship is distinguished from the procurator who administers the goods of another—generally of moral persons such as universities—outside of court affairs.[13] Bouuaert-Simenon give the following definition: *procurator designat illum qui in litibus personam gerit alterius non personaliter comparentis.*[14] However, it is permissible at times for the party to appear for himself, as provided for in Canon 1655, § 3.

The *decretum* of Gratian has the following definition of a postulator, that is, an advocate: *est autem postulare desiderium suum vel amici sui in iure apud eum, qui iurisdictioni praeest, exponere, vel desiderio contradicere.*[15] Reiffenstuel gives the same definition and adds that those who act as postulator in the name of another or for another are commonly called *advocati, patroni causarum, oratores, et causidici.*[16] Reiffenstuel also states that the office of advocate is public and honorable while that of procurator is private, onerous and not deserving of special honor.[17]

Since the definition of the glossators restricts the prohibition to acting *in iure sive in iudicio,* that is, in the court room, clerics are not forbidden to express the law or to give counsel even in writing to those who request it privately. In the courtroom, however, counsel is forbidden.[18]

Canon 139, § 3, provides explicitly for only two cases in which a cleric may act as procurator or advocate in a civil court, that is, when he is representing himself or his own church. Under the old

12 Canons 1655 to 1666.

13 Glossa f "procuratores," ad c. un., *de obligatis ad ratiocinia ordinandis vel non,* X, I, 19.

14 Bouuaert-Simenon, *Manuale,* I, n. 298.

15 C. 2, c. III, q. 7.

16 Reiffenstuel, lib. I, tit. 37, nn. 3, 4.

17 Reiffenstuel, lib. I, tit. 37, n. 6.

18 Pignatelli, *Consultationes,* IV, consult. 191, ad 3; Reiffenstuel, lib. I, tit. 37, n. 5; Fagnanus, lib. I, tit. 37, n. 20.

law explicit permission was also granted to act, without the permission of the ordinary, for relatives, if necessity demanded, or for other persons who needed their help, *pro coniunctis aut miserabilibus personis*. Modern authors dispute as to whether or not the last two exceptions are valid under the law of the Code. Ayrinhac, Cocchi, A Coronata, Maroto, Augustine, and Vidal maintain that clerics can act for relatives under the law of the Code.[19] The opposite opinion is held by Vermeersch-Creusen, De Meester, and Blat.[20] Vermeersch-Creusen base their opinion on the words *causa propria*, stating that they exclude the causes even of relatives. The opposing authors deny this, and their opinion seems to be more tenable.

Since it is doubtful, therefore, whether the new law differs from the old, the new law is to be interpreted according to the old law.[21] Thus is thrown open the question as to who were included where the old law permitted clerics to act *pro personis coniunctis*. Schmalzgrueber and Fagnanus contended that blood relations as far as the fourth degree were included. Fagnanus added that those related by affinity were likewise included—to the fourth degree, if the relationship arose from marital intercourse; otherwise, only to the second degree.[22] Fagnanus included under the *coniuncti* a very intimate friend.[23]

Acting for Persons in Distress

It is singular that most modern authors, who treat of whether or not clerics are allowed to act as procurator or advocate in civil courts for relatives under the law of the Code, do not treat of the question whether clerics are likewise allowed to act for persons in need as they were allowed under the old law. Of the modern authors who would allow clerics to act for relatives without the permission of the ordinary only Maroto and Ayrinhac treat the question of persons in need. They both agree that these latter are not to be

[19] Ayrinhac, *General Legislation,* 304, 305; Cocchi, *Commentarium,* II, 135; A Coronata, *Institutiones,* II, n. 202; Maroto, *Institutiones,* I, n. 568, B; Augustine, *Commentary,* II, 91; Wernz-Vidal, *De Personis,* n. 131, II, nota (57).

[20] Vermeersch-Creusen, *Epitome,* I, n. 223; De Meester, *Compendium,* I, 265; Blat, *Commentarium,* II, 101.

[21] Canon 6, 4°.

[22] Schmalzgrueber, lib. I, tit. 37, n. 8 ad 3; Fagnanus, lib. I, tit. 37, nn. 8, 9.

[23] Fagnanus, lib. I, tit. 37, n. 11.

represented by clerics under the law of the Code without the permission of the ordinary. They both maintain that this exception is not continued under the law of the Code, lest it give rise to abuses.[24] This seems the more correct stand because the authors who maintain that relatives are allowed to be represented by clerics under the law of the Code base their contention on the claim that relatives are included in the words *propria causa* found in Canon 139, § 3. On the other hand there is no such basis for persons in need, and this exception of past legislation seems to be definitely omitted.

Vermeersch-Creusen, De Meester, Blat—all of whom maintain that the permission of the ordinary must be had to represent even relatives—are consistent in stating that clerics are forbidden to act on their own accord for needy persons.[25]

Clerics Acting for Their Own Churches

Canon 139, § 3, states expressly that clerics may act in favor of their own church. By the word "church" is here meant that particular church in which the cleric has some office or benefice. Fagnanus mentions three cases in which a cleric may act by reason of this exception: (1) *ratione personae*—the church bringing suit against a layman who refuses to recognize the jurisdiction of the ecclesiastical courts may be represented as procurator or advocate by a cleric of this church; (2) *ratione delicti*—because of a sacrilege or some other crime of the mixed forum the church wishes to bring a layman before the secular courts. The provisions against acting in criminal matters involving grave personal punishment as explained in the following chapter must, however, be observed; (3) *ratione rei*—if the church is forced to enter suit in the secular courts to recover a thing which belongs to it, a cleric of the same church can act as representative.[26]

The decretalists mention two cases in which a cleric is forbidden

[24] Maroto, *Institutiones,* I, n. 568, B; Ayrinhac, *General Legislation,* pp. 304, 305.

[25] Vermeersch-Creusen, *Epitome,* I, n. 223; De Meester, *Compendium,* I, 265; Blat, *Commentarium,* II, 101.

[26] Fagnanus, lib. I, tit. 37, nn. 11, 12, 13.

to act as advocate or procurator: (1) Cases involving the penalty of death or mutilation, because of the danger of irregularity for the cleric. This irregularity is not found in the Code but clerics are, nevertheless, forbidden to enter such cases as is explained fully in the following chapter. (2) Cases against the church in which the cleric has a benefice, or against his own bishop, because of the ingratitude which would thus be shown. Schmalzgrueber claims, however, that the prohibition to act against one's own church must be taken *regulariter,* and he cites the following cases in which a cleric can so act: (1) If by precept of his superior he is ordered to do so. (2) If he represents himself or persons related to him. (3) If he acts for persons in need otherwise deprived of an advocate—this exception is doubtful under the Code as explained above. (4) If the cleric have a prelatial dignity in the church which he represents, whereas in the church against which he acts he enjoys merely a benefice. This latter is of no moment under the law of the Code, that is, as regards secular courts, since all clerics can act in ecclesiastical courts where cases of this kind would be brought.[27] Reiffenstuel, however, claims that a cleric cannot act against his own church even for a relative.[28] Of course, a cleric could not bring suit even for a relative against the church, or against a cleric, in the secular courts in contravention of the privilege of the ecclesiastical forum.

As regards churches in which the clerics has no office or benefice he cannot, without the permission of his own ordinary, act as procurator or advocate in the secular courts. This is true, likewise, for all pious causes which do not belong to his church.[29]

A cleric can act also for his associate clerics of the same church. This opinion is held by the glossators and by the decretalists. The clerics of the same church are more generally considered as exceptions because of their spiritual relationship which is to be acknowledged as stronger than the physical relationship of brothers.[30]

[27] Schmalzgrueber, lib. I, tit. 37, n. 9.

[28] Reiffenstuel, lib. I, tit. 37, n. 23.

[29] *Cf.* De Meester, *Compendium,* I, 265.

[30] Glossa *pro seipso,* c. 3, X, *de postulando,* I, 37; Fagnanus, lib. I, tit. 37, n. 10; Schmalzgrueber, lib. I, tit. 37, n. 10.

Stricter Law for Religious

Canon 1657, § 3, determines that religious must have the permission of their superior to act as procurator or advocate in *diocesan* courts even when they represent their own institute. *A fortiori*, therefore, if religious desire to act in the civil courts they must, in all cases, have the permission of their superior. Reiffenstuel expressed this same opinion as holding in his time.[81] At the same time he states that with the permission of the superior a religious can act in favor of those who have befriended his society. Those living a common life in imitation of religious, but without religious vows, are to be guided by the legislation enacted for religious in this matter.

Bishops and those enjoying an equal dignity should not act as procurators or advocates.

Capuchin Friars Minor and other Friars Minor cannot be an advocate or procurator for their own society since they can possess nothing of their own even in common. Their possessions are held in the name of the Holy See.[82]

Dispensations

The Sacred Congregation of the Council, in 1883, allowed a Spanish priest to act as advocate in the secular courts with the provision that all scandal be absent and that the priest either abstain completely from criminal matters or write and act only for the defense. This concession was granted *pro gratia et ad tempus episcopo benevisum, facto verbo cum Ssmo.* On the testimony of the bishop the priest was skilled, needed the income, and had promised to defend the immunities and rights of the Church and of clerics.[83] The sacred congregation, as it expressly stated, followed the teaching of Benedict XIV in this regard, who indicates that similar papal indults in his time were not unknown. He adds, however, that once the priest has gained sufficient income the bishop should understand that he has the authority to revoke the exercise

[81] Reiffenstuel, lib. I, tit. 37, n. 24.

[82] Canon 582, §2; Schäfer, *De Religiosis*, p. 323; Reiffenstuel, lib. I, tit. 37, n. 26.

[83] S. C. C., *Nullius Clunien.*, 4 aug., 1883—*ASS*, XVI (1883-1884), 227-230.

of the indult, as is also true if the priest should so conduct himself as to give offense or scandal.[34]

In the same text quoted in the preceding paragraph Benedict XIV pointed out that such indults were never granted to religious and so a superior today would hardly be justified in allowing a religious such a general permission.

As regards clerics attending lay universities for the study of civil law the ordinary must report to Rome if such clerics are observing the rules of the Sacred Congregation of the Consistory and he must state the number of clerics engaged in such studies.[35]

Violation Causes a Simple Impediment to Orders

It seems beyond doubt that any cleric or religious acting against the prohibition of serving as procurator or advocate in civil courts, as explained, contracts the simple impediment to orders listed in Canon 987, 3°. Cappello refers to the whole of Canon 139 as containing occupations from which this impediment arises.[36] Hickey maintains the same position.[37]

Before the Code it was likewise the opinion of authors that this simple impediment arose from all occupations forbidden to clerics.[38] A more detailed discussion of the consequences of this impediment is found on pages 4 to 7. A treatment of the penal sanctions of Canon 2379 is had on pages 17 and 18.

[34] Benedict XIV, *De Synodo Dioecesana,* XIII, 10, 12.

[35] S. C. Consist., *Formula servanda in relationibus dioecesanis conficiendis,* 4 nov., 1918, n. 50—*AAS,* X (1918), 496.

[36] Cappello, *De Sacra Ordinatione,* n. 521.

[37] Hickey, John J., *Irregularities and Simple Impediments in the New Code of Canon Law,* The Catholic University of America, Canon Law Studies, n. 7, Washington: The Catholic University of America, 1920, pp. 76, 77.

[38] Reiffenstuel, lib. I, tit. 19, nn. 2, 3, 5, 6; Gasparri, *De Sacra Ordinatione,* I, n. 553.

CHAPTER VII

ENGAGING IN CIVIL CRIMINAL TRIALS

Canon 139, § 3. Sine licentia sui Ordinarii . . . [clerici] in laicali iudicio criminali, gravem personalem poenam prosequente nullam partem habeant, ne testimonium quidem sine necessitate ferentes.

The final prohibition contained in Canon 139, § 3, forbids clerics, without the consent of their own ordinary, to take any part in criminal cases of the civil law involving grave personal punishments, and even to give testimony in such cases, except when compelled by some necessity. As pointed out on pages 2 to 4 the word cleric here includes also religious and those living a common life in imitation of religious, but without vows.

Historical Conspectus

From the days of the Christian emperors bishops were freed from the obligation of testifying in civil cases and the judge was directed to send a subordinate officer to the bishop that the latter might, in a way befitting the episcopal dignity, state upon the holy gospels what he knew concerning the facts in the case. The bishop was not required to take an oath.[1]

It appears, however, that priests and other members of the clergy were not exempt from testifying either in civil or criminal cases. Priests were exempt from the torture which was sometimes applied in securing testimony. They were subject to legal action for deceit if, taking advantage of their immunity from physical force, they should conceal the truth. It seems that the clergy inferior to the priesthood were subjected to all the rigors of the law in force for lay people.[2]

[1] Codex (1.3), 7; Novellae 123, 7, 8.

[2] Codex (1.3), 8.

Later a provision was made that if priests or deacons were convicted of giving false testimony and the case be one involving money, they were to be excluded from the divine ministry for a period of three years and were to be confined to a monastery as a means of punishment. In criminal cases, however, priests and deacons were to be deprived of their clerical honors and punished with the full penalties of the law. Members of the lower clergy giving false testimony in either a pecuniary or criminal case were to be expelled from their ecclesiastical offices and subjected to blows.[3]

Although in the Middle Ages clerics were allowed to assist the king in the ministration of justice, they were not allowed so to act when there existed danger of the effusion of blood, that is, of death or bodily dismemberment or flogging, and the prohibition was enforced with the penalty of immediate loss of office.[4]

Alexander III (1159-1181) added a penalty of excommunication, if after a warning the cleric did not cease to act in these cases.[5] In the Third General Council of the Lateran, 1179, the same Pope repeated the previous legislation and added that clerics were not to be present at the execution of penalties leading to the effusion of blood; neither could clerics dictate or write letters required for the carrying out of such penalties.[6]

The Council of London, 1268, forbade clerics the office of advocate in cases involving the effusion of blood, and if a cleric should aid the prosecution in such a case he would incur *ipso facto* a suspension from office; an additional punishment, to be determined by the superior, was to be inflicted on one acting as a judge or his assistant.[7] Boniface VIII (1294-1303) provided that any cleric having temporal jurisdiction could delegate a lay person to hear criminal cases and, even if in the carrying out of justice a penalty

[3] Novellae 123, 20.

[4] Fourth Council of Toledo (633), c. 31—Mansi, X, 628; Eleventh Council of Toledo (675), c. 6—Mansi, XI, 141; c. 29, 30, C. XXIII, q. 8; Council of London (1175), c. 3—Mansi, XXII, 148.

[5] C. 5, X, *ne clerici vel monachi saecularibus negotiis se immisceant,* III, 50.

[6] C. 9, X, *ne clerici vel monachi saecularibus negotiis se immisceant,* III, 50.

[7] C. 6—Mansi, XXIII, 1222.

of effusion of blood was passed, the cleric so delegating would not become irregular.[8]

An instruction of the Holy Office, 1866, shows that the punishment of irregularity was still in force for clerics personally engaging in such cases.[9]

A later response from the Holy Office under date of the 27th of August, 1902, is of importance and requires careful interpretation. A massacre of the Christians in a foreign mission had occurred and seven of the attackers had been captured. After a trial six of them were decapitated and a seventh had fled. The Holy Office stated that even though the missionaries had acted as plaintiffs in the prosecution of the case no irregularity was incurred, and that they could continue the case against the fugitive, provided that this be necessary to repair the harm done, or to prevent others from committing similar outrages. Otherwise they could not continue the case. The Holy Office further stated that if a similar case should arise in the future another trial would be licit under the same circumstances.[10] This clearly shows the opinion of the Holy Office that the prohibition against clerics taking part in trials involving the effusion of blood is not to be considered as depriving them of the protection afforded by the civil law.

Law of the Code

Since Canon 139, § 3, retains all the old law it might be helpful to summarize the actions in criminal trials which were expressly forbidden before the promulgation of the Code. Clerics could not assist in the ministration of justice when there existed danger of the effusion of blood, that is, of death, of mutilation and of flogging. They were not to dictate or write letters required for the carrying out of such penalties, nor should they be present at the infliction of these punishments. They could not act as an advocate,

[8] C. 3, *ne clerici vel monachi saecularibus negotiis se immisceant,* III, 24, in VI°.

[9] S. C. S. Off., instr. *(pro Vic. Ap. ad Gallas),* 20 iun., 1866, ad 21—*Fontes,* n. 994.

[10] S. C. S. Off. (*Chen-si Merid.*), 27 aug., 1902—*Fontes,* n. 1260.

nor as a judge, nor as his assistant. As will be developed later, the provisions regarding irregularity and penal sanctions have been somewhat mitigated by the Code. All the aforesaid offices have been considered opposed to the spirit of mildness and forgiveness, which characterizes the priesthood, and are looked upon as being detrimental to the good name of clerics among the people.

The legislator is assuming that the trials spoken of here are just trials. If the trial should be unjust then all those who coöperate share also in the guilt of imposing a punishment unjustly. If a death sentence is actually carried out then the coöperators would be guilty of voluntary homicide and would incur the irregularity and all the sanctions of the Code provided for this crime.

According to the decretalists, clerics and even bishops could impose the punishment of confinement, for example, in a monastery.[11]

Canon 139, § 3, enacts a broader prohibition than is found in the law hitherto in that it includes not only cases of the effusion of blood but also those cases involving grave personal punishment which would seem to include a penitentiary sentence. Interpreters of the Code agree that a personal punishment includes confinement in a penitentiary; Vermeersch-Creusen state that a personal punishment is one opposed to a punishment involving the payment of a fine.[12] The latter is the usual form of punishment imposed in criminal matters which can be considered as not directed in the person of the accused. It affects his goods rather than his person. Some modern jurisdictions do impose the penalty of stripes and this, of course, is to be considered a personal punishment.

Must the element of time be considered to determine that confinement to a penitentiary constitutes a *grave* personal punishment? Bouuaert-Simenon express an affirmative response, by indicating that an incarceration of some length is required.[13] Other authors do not consider the element of time. The difficulty is best settled, perhaps, by a distinction. Even the lightest of penitentiary sentences would be a grave personal punishment for a person who had

[11] Schmalzgrueber, lib. III, tit. 50, n. 37; Pirhing, lib. III, tit. 50, n. 13.

[12] *Cf.* Augustine, *Commentary,* II, 91; Bouuaert-Simenon, *Manuale,* I, n. 298, 3; Vermeersch-Creusen, *Epitome,* I, n. 223.

[13] Bouuaert-Simenon, *Manuale,* I, n. 298, 3.

never suffered such a penalty in the past, whereas for an habitual criminal a confinement of some length would be necessary to constitute a *grave* personal punishment. A Coronata and Maroto would appeal to secular legislation for a criterion to determine whether or not a certain punishment is to be considered grave.[14] Such criterions can hardly be found in American civil law, and the same commentary would hold whether the fault be termed technically a felony or merely a misdemeanor.

The law of the Code does not require the permission of the ordinary to testify in a correctional court. However, at times particular statutes are more severe.[15]

Since the Code forbids a cleric to take any part in these criminal trials, he should not act as court interpreter without previous permission of the ordinary.

Witnesses in Criminal Trials

The necessity to give testimony of which the canon speaks could arise first of all from the demands of the civil law. The cleric should request to be excused, but should the authorities insist, he may testify without the permission of the ordinary. Vermeersch-Creusen alone differ from this opinion and they would limit the necessity to that arising from the law of charity to defend a party from injustice.[16]

Furthermore, the moral necessity for a cleric to testify in favor of the accused—either as to facts or as to his character—in order to protect him from an injustice would seem always to be a sufficient cause.[17] This is the opinion of the majority of canonists, yet, Blat and Cocchi would demand previous permission from the ordinary before testimony could be lawfully given.[18] In practice, therefore,

[14] A Coronata, *Institutiones,* I, n. 202, footnote 6; Maroto, *Institutiones,* n. 568, B, note 4.

[15] Bouuaert-Simenon, *Manuale,* I, n. 298, 3.

[16] Vermeersch-Creusen, *Epitome,* I, n. 223; Wernz-Vidal, *De Personis,* n. 131, II; Blat, *De Personis,* p. 101; Maroto, *Institutiones,* n. 568, B; Cocchi, *Commentarium,* II, 135; Augustine, *Commentary,* II, 92; Ayrinhac, *General Legislation,* n. 299. The last two authors say that it is proper and commendable to notify the ordinary if time allows.

[17] Maroto, *Institutiones,* n. 568, B; Wernz-Vidal, *De Personis,* n. 131, II; Vermeersch-Creusen, *Epitome,* I, n. 223; Ayrinhac, *General Legislation,* n. 299.

[18] Blat, *Commentarium,* II, 101; Cocchi, *Commentarium,* II, 135.

a cleric could testify in such cases of necessity without permission of the ordinary. Necessity might also arise from physical force or fear imposed by an interested party. In this case the ordinary should be informed if time and circumstances permit.

The authors fail to consider the possibility of the necessity of a cleric giving testimony against the accused in favor of a third party. For instance a cleric may know of evidence, which is necessary and which he alone can supply, to protect the fortune or good name of an innocent person against the usurpation or calumnies of the accused, even though such testimony would result in a lengthy penitentiary sentence for the guilty party. Again, in time of war a cleric may have knowledge—speaking always of the external forum, of course—of the activities of spies, and his testimony in the military court would be necessary to protect the nation against serious loss. In these cases, too, the necessity of testifying arising from the law of charity would seem to give the cleric the right to testify without the permission of the ordinary, although it would be advisable to consult him if time is had.

The desire to repair the damage done to society by the crime of the accused is clearly not sufficient reason to testify without the consent of the ordinary.

The decretalists and the glossators were agreed that clerics, although forbidden to be present at criminal trials involving the penalty of the loss of blood, or mutilation, or decapitation, were not made irregular nor were to be deposed unless they were present in an authoritative manner or in some way aided in the sentence. However, a cleric attending such a trial merely as a spectator was acting contrary to the spirit of the clerical state and should be punished.[19]

Since Canon 139, § 3, forbids taking any part in the criminal trial, it would seem at first sight that the giving of counsel outside of the court room would not be strictly included in the prohibition. However, since there would be danger that the giving of such advice might become known publicly to the detriment of clerical reverence

[19] *Cf.* Schmalzgrueber, lib. III, tit. 50, n. 38; Pirhing, lib. III, tit. 5, n. 12; Reiffenstuel, lib. III, tit. 50, n. 21; also glossa, *sanguinis,* c. 9, X, *ne clerici vel monachi saecularibus negotiis se immisceant,* III, 50.

among the people, it would certainly be advisable to abstain from the giving of advice in these cases. Reiffenstuel maintains—without making clear whether he is speaking of giving counsel *in iudicium* or *extra iudicium,* but probably meaning the latter—that a cleric could respond in general to an inquirer by saying that a certain crime is to be punished by this particular penalty, or the cleric could point out the law in the sources.[20]

Irregularities

In the law of the Code, with the exception of the judge who condemns the accused to death, no irregularity is incurred by those who take part in these trials.[21] However, clerics are forbidden to attend these trials by virtue of the past interpretation of the prohibition contained in Canon 139, § 3, forbidding them to have any part in such criminal cases. If his presence or actions should prejudice the judge against the accused the cleric would offend, in a lesser degree, of course, but much after the manner of the individual who is present in a lynching mob without taking any actual part in the crime itself.

Under the law of the Code a judge pronouncing the sentence of death even though it be a just one is irregular *ex defectu,* as such an act is considered against the spirit of mildness of the clerical state.[22] Since the Code is silent concerning the irregularities of past legislation, which affected the various coöperators in such a trial, they must be considered as abrogated.[23]

Does the judge incur this irregularity, if, after sentence of death is pronounced by him, the criminal escapes or his sentence is commuted by a higher authority? The general opinion is to the effect that the irregularity is not incurred. This opinion is held by Pirhing, Wernz, Gasparri and Cappello.[24] Their argument is based

[20] Reiffenstuel, lib. III, tit. 50, n. 13.

[21] *Cf.* Canon 984, 6°.

[22] Canon 984, 6°.

[23] Canon 983.

[24] Pirhing, lib. III, tit. 5, n. 13; Wernz, *Ius Decretalium,* II, n. 123; Gasparri, *De Sacra Ordinatione,* I, n. 451; Cappello, *De Sacra Ordinatione,* n. 497, 5. The latter maintains that this opinion approximates more closely to a true interpretation of the law.

on the purpose of the law, that is, the safeguarding of the esteem and reverence for the clerical state among the people, which would suffer injury if candidates were freely admitted to the clerical status after their hands had been tainted, as it were, with the spilling of blood. As long, therefore, as the sentence of death is not actually carried out no irregularity follows.

The arguments for the opposite opinion [25] may be summed up as follows:

1. Canon 984, 6°, states merely that the judge who passes the sentence of death is irregular and makes no mention of the carrying out of the sentence. This argument is strengthened by the fact that the very next canon states expressly that none of those who attempt or coöperate in an abortion are irregular unless the effect actually follows. The fact that Canon 984, 6°, makes no mention of the carrying out of the effect indicates that it is not required to incur the penalty.[26]

2. The argument deduced from the aim of the law by those who maintain that the irregularity is not incurred unless the sentence is actually carried out seems rather to favor the opposite opinion. The irregularity is imposed because the condemning to death is opposed to the spirit of forgiveness and mildness which should characterize the clerical state. The fact that the sentence is not put into effect is not attributable *per se* to the judge, and the force of his action is not thereby mitigated. This last opinion seems to be the more probable one.

The irregularity remains doubtful. While a dispensation *ad cautelam* would be granted readily for a lay judge, it is altogether likely, if not admittedly certain, that the Holy See would be much stricter in regard to a cleric who has passed the death sentence.[27]

[25] Vidal differs from Wernz in maintaining this opinion—*cf.* Wernz-Vidal, *De Rebus,* n. 243, II; Hickey also holds that the carrying out of the sentence is not required to incur the irregularity: Hickey, *Irregularities and Simple Impediments,* p. 42.

[26] Canon 985, 4°; *cf.* also Canon 2350, § 1; *cf.* Canon 18 for the value of such an argument from parallel legislation.

[27] For a treatment of the regulations concerning doubtful irregularities *cf.* Cappello, *De Sacra Ordinatione,* n. 439, and other approved authors.

Is a judge liable to incur this irregularity when he functions as a member of a collegiate tribunal? If the majority vote is against the death sentence, then a cleric or layman voting for capital punishment is not thereby made irregular, for the death sentence is only voted upon without being actually pronounced. If the majority vote favors the imposition of the death sentence a divided opinion is held regarding the irregularity of the minority voter or voters. The first opinion holds that all are irregular: (1) Because the vote is a secret one, the judges acting *per modum unius,* and the faithful have no way of knowing who voted against the death sentence. (2) Because an irregularity *ex delicto* is not involved, but an irregularity *ex defectu.* In other words, the irregularity is imposed because of the resultant diminution of esteem and reverence among the faithful, and not because of any delict on the part of the cleric or layman.

The second opinion would exempt the minority voter or voters from the irregularity. Cappello says the first opinion is the more acceptable one, although he admits that the second one is probable.[28] Wernz and Gasparri, writing before the promulgation of the Code, maintained that the collegiate judges were all irregular.[29] Concerning pre-Code writers it must be remembered that in the law of that time the irregularity included many of those who took part in the trial besides the judge who is the only one included in the law of the Code. This fact may have influenced the opinion of some of these authors. It is perhaps for this reason that Vidal[30] differs from Wernz by holding that only those who vote in favor of capital punishment are irregular. The opinion of Gasparri, however, cannot be set aside so lightly, because he expressly states that the reason why all the judges of the tribunal are irregular rests in the fact that they act *per modum unius.*

In view of the reasons stated above and considering the aim of the law it would seem that all the members of the tribunal become irregular, although the other opinion is not without some authority.

A judge or judges on a court of appeal are not made irregular

[28] Cappello, *De Sacra Ordinatione,* n. 497, 2.

[29] Wernz, *Ius Decretalium,* II, n. 123; Gasparri, *De Sacra Ordinatione,* I, n. 453, a.

[30] Wernz-Vidal, *De Rebus,* n. 245, II.

by declaring that in the trial and imposition of the death sentence there occurred no defect of the law. Such action as regards the death sentence is only indirect. The same may be said in favor of a ruler who refused to commute the death sentence.[31] If the appeal is made, not on the basis of mercy, but on the legal merits of the case, a cleric acting as a ruler should place the appeal before a delegate.

Clerics acting as secular rulers or among a group of legislators are not forbidden to enact the punishment of death for certain crimes and are not thereby made irregular, if through the force of these laws a court applies the extreme penalty. They concur only remotely. The same may be said of a cleric voting in his capacity as a private citizen in favor of imposing capital punishment for certain crimes.[32]

This irregularity is likewise not incurred by a bishop who degrades a cleric for a grievous crime and then hands him over to the secular authorities who pass the sentence of death.[33]

Jury Service

According to the more common opinion a cleric acting on a jury would not incur the irregularity.[34] The arguments of these authors may be summed up as follows: (1) The jury considers only the facts and circumstances of the crime and the consequent guilt of the accused, but in no sense can they be said to pronounce the death sentence. (2) From the fact that the judges of the Inquisition did not become irregular in turning over heretics who were executed by the secular arm, Gasparri argues to a parallel conclusion that the jurymen are free from such irregularity. The weight of these arguments will be considered later. Wernz maintained that the jurymen

[31] Wernz, *Ius Decretalium,* II, n. 125; Gasparri, *De Sacra Ordinatione,* I, n. 454, g and h.

[32] Gasparri, *De Sacra Ordinatione,* I, n. 454, a; Wernz, *Ius Decretalium,* II, n. 125; Schmalzgrueber, lib. III, tit. 50, n. 38.

[33] Gasparri, *De Sacra Ordinatione,* I, n. 454, c.

[34] Ayrinhac, *Legislation on the Sacraments,* p. 367, 6°; Wernz-Vidal, *De Rebus,* n. 245, II; Aertnys-Damen, *Theologia Moralis,* II, n. 602; Cappello, *De Sacra Ordinatione,* n. 497, 1; Gasparri, *De Sacra Ordinatione,* I, n. 454, c.

are irregular but his opinion is of little value under the law of the Code, as he includes the jurymen among other coöperators, all of whom were irregular before the Code.[35]

At this point it might be well to analyze briefly the influence which a jury exercises in the passing of a death sentence, particularly in many jurisdictions in the United States. First of all the jury passes on the facts, and then brings in a verdict of guilty with no recommendation for mercy, whereupon the law (in some states) operates automatically in requiring the judge to pronounce sentence of death, without allowing him any alternative in the matter. In such a procedure the influence of the jury is at its maximum, that is, just short of the actual pronouncement of the death sentence, which is hardly found in modern court practice. While keeping in mind the aim of the law, one might with considerable reason urge that under circumstances such as these the jurymen would contract the irregularity. In the case as proposed the judge is acting as an agent in a merely passive rôle. In reality the sentence of death is determined by the verdict of the jury and its pronouncement is authorized by their mandate. The lack of lenity and the want of forbearance which, *per se,* offend against the spirit of forgiveness are, then, lodged with the jury. The feelings of the people would be directed in opposition to them rather than against the judge.

It must be borne in mind, of course, that in order to incur the irregularity service on the jury must be voluntary. Otherwise the action would not be a grave sin and, by virtue of Canon 986, no irregularity would arise. In the absence of positive legislation in the United States clergymen have been held not to be exempt from jury duty.[36] All the members of the jury panel are given an opportunity to request an exemption from jury duty and the judge has broad discretionary powers to pass on the merits of the requests for exemption. Should the judge refuse to excuse the cleric in spite of his protests, the cleric would not be serving voluntarily and the irregularity would clearly not be incurred.

In a case where the verdict of the jury compels the judge to pronounce the death sentence, as outlined above, a question of

[35] Wernz, *Ius Decretalium,* II, n. 125.

[36] Zollmann, *American Church Law,* p. 52.

terminology is involved. Canon 984, 6°, declares irregular a judge *qui mortis sententiam tulit*. Does the word *tulit* connote only the *pronouncing* of the sentence [37] or does it imply the *actual imposition* or *authoritative determination* of the sentence? If the latter be true, then in the above case the judge would escape the irregularity, while the jurymen might be said at least to impose effectively the death sentence. The authors hardly seem to consider the above case, which is not at all uncommon in the United States. Vidal for instance speaks of the jury's verdict as *influencing* the sentence to be proferred by the judge.[38] In this case, though, the verdict *determines* the opinion of the judge. Gasparri likewise speaks of the judge weighing the verdict of the jury and then deciding on the punishment of death.[39] In other words, these authors seem to presuppose that the judge enjoys the power of rendering alternative sentences under the guidance of the law. In such a case their opinion is undoubtedly correct.

Gasparri, as stated above, likewise draws a parallel between the judges of the Inquisition and the members of a jury. He argues that the inquisitors were not considered irregular, because they did not pronounce the punishment of death but only determined the existence of the crime and the guilt of the accused. The latter was then turned over to the civil authorities who applied the punishment provided in the civil criminal code for such a crime.[40] However, the parallel hardly withstands an analysis. The inquisitors were acting in an ecclesiastical court and treating of a matter primarily ecclesiastical, while the jury is acting in a civil criminal court and treating of a matter involving primarily the disturbance of the social order.

As a summary it would seem, therefore, that if the judge is given an alternative between a death sentence and a milder one, then the jurymen are clearly not thereby irregular if he chooses the severer penalty. If, however, the judge is given no choice and the jury's verdict automatically demands the death sentence, then the irregularity as affecting the judge might be considered doubtful. In

[37] Wernz uses the verb *pronuntiare:* Wernz, *Ius Decretalium*, II, n. 123.

[38] Wernz-Vidal, *De Rebus*, n. 245, II.

[39] Gasparri, *De Sacra Ordinatione*, I, n. 454, c.

[40] Gasparri, *De Sacra Ordinatione*, I, n. 454, c.

view of the aim of the law one might be inclined to the opinion that the jurymen in such a case would become irregular. However, *finis legis non est lex,* and since the canon restricts itself to those who at least pronounce the death sentence the jurymen do not incur the irregularity. If one embraced the opposite opinion, then, if an unanimous decision on the part of the jury be not required—it is required at present in all jurisdictions of the United States—the commentary as outlined above in regard to collegiate judges is to be applied.

A cleric who acts as a judge, or on a jury, indicting an accused person for trial does not contract an irregularity, even though the accused be eventually executed. The concurrence in the death sentence is only remote.[41]

Since the Code is silent in regard to prosecuting attorneys and other officials and coöperators in the trial, these cannot be considered subject to an irregularity.

Cases in Which Clerics May Act

By virtue of the reply of the Holy Office—the details of which are found above on page 46—clerics are not forbidden to press a criminal action in the civil courts against murderers provided that this be necessary to repair the harm done or to prevent others from committing such crimes. Particular statutes may be stricter and in the United States the bishop must pass on such matters.[42]

In view of past legislation the ordinary would not be justified in allowing a cleric to act as judge, juryman, prosecuting attorney or an assistant attorney against the accused in a criminal trial involving a grave personal punishment. The Holy See has not customarily granted such permissions in the past. Benedict XIV speaks of indults allowing clerics, otherwise deprived of sufficient income, to act as advocates in criminal cases provided they act and write only for the defense.[43]

Under the old law a cleric acting as advocate even for the accused

[41] Gasparri, *De Sacra Ordinatione,* I, n. 454, a.

[42] *Concilii Plenarii Baltimorensis II Acta et Decreta,* nn. 155, 156.

[43] Benedict XIV, *De Synodo Dioecesana,* XIII, 10, 12.

ran the risk of incurring the irregularity which arose if the latter should be decapitated or mutilated because of the cleric's lack of skill. For this reason Fagnanus and Hostiensis state that a cleric should not act even for the defense.[44]

Schmalzgrueber says that it is safer for a cleric not to act as an attorney, but probably it is not prohibited.[45] Since the Code states that clerics are to have *no part* in criminal trials they must have permission of their ordinary to act as procurator or advocate even for the accused.[46] Considering the above opinions and the removal of the danger of irregularity under the law of the Code the ordinary would seem to be justified, for example, in granting permission for a cleric to act as advocate or procurator in his own defense or in defense of his relatives in criminal matters.[47]

[44] Fagnanus, lib. III, tit. 50, n. 23; Hostiensis, lib. III, tit. 50, n. 6.

[45] Schmalzgrueber, lib. III, tit. 50, n. 9.

[46] *Cf.* Blat, *Commentarium,* II, 101; Cocchi, *Commentarium,* II, 135.

[47] The preceding chapter of this dissertation contains more details in regard to clerics acting as procurators or advocates in secular courts.

CHAPTER VIII

LEGISLATIVE OFFICES

Canon 139, § 4. Senatorum aut oratorum legibus ferendis, quos *deputatos* vocant, munus [clerici] ne sollicitent neve acceptent sine licentia Sanctae Sedis in locis ubi pontificia prohibitio intercesserit; idem ne attentent aliis in locis sine licentia tum sui Ordinarii, tum Ordinarii loci in quo electio facienda est.

Historical Notes

Since only with the establishment of democratic systems of government could the question arise of clerics serving as deputies to parliamentary gatherings, the historical conspectus of paragraph four of Canon 139 is rather confined. However, as early as 1658, Alexander VII took occasion to forbid forcibly secular pastors and regulars to take part in any way in matters pertaining to secular politics; nor could they propose anyone for public office even though such a one be best equipped for the office; the presence of clerics at meetings or conventions treating of public matters was likewise prohibited.[1] A year later the Sacred Congregation for the Propagation of the Faith took occasion to repeat this prohibition in a lengthy instruction.[2]

Ten years later Clement IX repeated verbatim this legislation of his predecessor.[3]

With Leo XIII a more liberal policy is advocated. Democratic systems of government offer indeed a peaceful means of defending the

[1] Alexander VII, const. "*Sacrosancti,*" 18 ian., 1658, § 12, n. VIII—*Fontes,* n. 235.

[2] S. C. de Prop. Fide, instr. (*ad Vic. Ap. Societ. Mission. ad Exteros*), a. 1659—*Fontes,* n. 4463.

[3] Clemens IX, const. "*In excelsa,*" 13 sept., 1669, par. 1, n. VIII—*Fontes,* n. 244.

rights of the Church, and the concentrated efforts of the Church became necessary to offset the organized attacks of which she was being made the victim. For this reason Leo's policy is worthy of study. While giving warning that clerics should not neglect their interior perfection in the study of civil and political matters, he urged that they should under the guidance of their bishops firmly defend the rights of the Church. To this end he advises the bishops of Hungary to call conventions to discuss not only the general work and needs of the Church, but also to aid and develop legislators of religious convictions and probity of life in defending the liberty of the Church. In forceful language he urges bishops by means of books and magazines and other writings to counteract strenuously the poisonous doctrines which were leading multitudes away from Christian life.[4]

Under Pius X is found the first concession allowing clerics, secular and regular, to be candidates for political office. This could be done only with the permission of their own ordinary and of the ordinary of the place where they wished to place themselves as candidates. This disposition was directed to France by the Sacred Congregation for Extraordinary Ecclesiastical Affairs acting with the express consent of the Holy Father, and is worded not as a concession but as a restraint.[5] A decree in 1913 declared this disposition to be still in effect for all clerics and by order of the Holy Father was made public law.[6]

Law of the Code

The Code practically repeats the legislation of the above paragraph, but expressly declares that the permission of the Holy See is required in those places where a pontifical prohibition is in force against clerics soliciting or accepting legislative offices. In other places the permission of the cleric's own ordinary and that of the

[4] Leo XIII, ep. encycl., *"Constanti Hungarorum,"* 2 sept., 1893, ad 5, 9—*Fontes,* n. 620.

[5] "De clericis candidatis in proximis electionibus ad Deputatorum comitia in Gallia," 2 apr., 1906—*ASS,* XXXIX (1906), 192.

[6] S. C. Consist., decr. 9 maii, 1913—*Fontes,* n. 2086.

ordinary of the place in which the election is to take place are necessary. As pointed out on pages 2 to 4 the word cleric here includes also religious and those living a common life in imitation of religious, but without vows.

A pontifical prohibition against clerics being candidates for legislative offices was in force in Italy up to the time of the Lateran Pact, 1929, when it was abrogated. The permission of the ordinary is sufficient at present.[7] Vermeersch-Creusen and Ayrinhac state such a prohibition existed in Bosnia-Herzegovina, which country, however, was incorporated into Yugoslavia in the settlement following the World War.[8] Ayrinhac states that such a prohibition existed (1923) in France but this statement seems without foundation.[9] An examination of the concordats now in force leads to the conclusion that there are no countries at present in which a cleric must have the permission of the Holy See in order to solicit or accept a public office as senator or deputy.

In order to solicit or accept such offices the cleric must have first of all the permission of his own ordinary. Religious must request the permission of a superior with the powers of an ordinary. Larraona maintains that the major superiors of non-exempt clerical religious organizations have the powers of ordinaries as regards this law.[10]

Besides the permission of his own ordinary the Code requires the permission of the ordinary of the place in which the election is to take place. A secular cleric, therefore, presenting himself to the electorate within his own diocese needs only the one permission of his own ordinary. A religious and those under the same discipline as religious must have a double permission. A secular cleric would also have need of a double permission if he desired to leave his own diocese and present himself to the electorate in another diocese.

[7] *Cf.* art. IV of the Lateran Pact— *AAS,* XXI (1929), 277, 278; Cappello, *Summa Iuris Canonici,* I, n. 245, 7.

[8] Vermeersch-Creusen, *Epitome,* I, n. 223, A, 3; Ayrinhac, *General Legislation,* n. 299.

[9] Ayrinhac, *General Legislation,* n. 299; *cf.* Mothon, *Institutions Canoniques,* I, n. 248, who says that France (1922) is under the common law in this regard.

[10] Arcadius Larraona, "Quaestio Canonica"—*Commentarium pro Religiosis,* IV (1923), 113-119.

The law, however, does not contemplate a situation in which the electorate is spread over a number of dioceses. This can be deduced from the fact that in referring to the *ordinary* of the place the singular person is employed. A double solution is possible, namely, either to secure the permission of all the local ordinaries in which the election is to be held, or the solution favored by A Coronata, Chelodi, and Cappello, that it is sufficient to procure the permission only of the ordinary of the place in which the center of the election is focused.[11]

It is somewhat difficult to draw an exact picture of the situation contemplated by these authors. They speak of securing the permission of the *Ordinarius loci centralis,* the *Ordinarius loci in quo centrum electionis ex lege est.* They refer probably to a district in which most of the voters are in a town of some size located in one diocese, whilst the minority of voters are from an outlying rural district in another diocese. Perhaps the latter voters have to cast their ballots in the town itself or perhaps, too, they may do so in some place within their own diocese. In any event it would seem that according to the opinion of the authors, in both of these cases the permission of the ordinary of the place in which the vast majority of the voters are domiciled is sufficient. This opinion is at least probable and has the support of a number of authors, but the opinion demanding the permission of all the ordinaries is also probable.

Another situation, common in this country, presents itself immediately for consideration. What is to be considered the center of election in a populous state wherein are situated two or more dioceses? Would a cleric desirous of presenting himself as a candidate for the Senate of the United States have to secure the permission of all the ordinaries? Would the permission of the majority of the ordinaries be sufficient? Could a single negative vote overrule the decision of the other ordinaries? Even a more complicated condition could arise in a country such as Italy, for example, where deputies are to be elected to represent certain classes of people spread throughout the land. Unless a definite decision is rendered

[11] A Coronata, *Institutiones,* I, n. 202; Chelodi, *Ius de Personis,* n. 121, f; Cappello, *Summa Iuris Canonici,* I, n. 245, 7.

by the Holy See it would seem that, in practice at least, the permission of the ordinaries with a decided majority of the electors within their jurisdiction would be sufficient. To suggest a definite percentage would be arbitrary. This is the liberal opinion and, since it is not contrary to the Code, may be followed. However the other opinion is just as probable. The matter should be settled amicably, of course, if possible. If this is not feasible then, if time permits, recourse should be had to the Holy See for a definite decision.

Canon 139, § 4, forbids first of all the soliciting of the office of senator or representative. By soliciting is meant the conducting of oneself as a candidate, or presenting one's name as a candidate to the proper authorities. Secondly, it forbids the *accepting* of these offices by which is meant not only the acceptance of an office to which one has been elected with or without one's own consent, but also the permitting of another to propose one's name as a candidate.

Appointment to Legislative Offices

Does the Code provide also for a situation in which a cleric could be *appointed* to the office of senator or representative? Frequently appointments are made in this country to fill the unexpired terms of deceased officials. From the mere wording of Canon 139, § 4, it would seem that the legislator is contemplating the necessity of an election, but in view of past history of the legislation on public office and the intention of the legislator, it would seem that a cleric would need the permission of his own ordinary to solicit or to accept an appointment to these positions. In this way only could the interests of the Church be safeguarded. Would he need the permission of other ordinaries? If he is not to represent the people of his own diocese it would seem that he would need the permission of the ordinary of the place he is to represent. A religious would need the permission of the ordinary of the place he is to represent. If the cleric is to represent people spread over a number of other dioceses the same commentary is to be applied as given above when the cleric must undergo an election.

In the early history of the United States clergymen were made ineligible for election to one or both branches of the legislature by constitutional provisions in a number of states. The fear of ecclesiastical domination of political affairs has long since been recognized as unjustified and in new constitutions such ineligibility has been dropped, and now only Maryland and Tennessee, by constitutions adopted respectively in 1867 and 1870, forbid legislative offices to the clergy.[12]

Canon 139, § 4, contains the only legislation in the Code directly affecting political activity on the part of clerics. According to Bouuaert-Simenon and Vermeersch-Creusen the prohibition of clerics taking part *in politicis contentionibus* was removed from the original draft of Canon 141, § 1, lest the Code seem to be desirous of preventing clerics from taking any part in political discussions which might at times be necessary for the welfare of the Church and the people.[13] In past history priests have held office in the national congressional body of the United States. Similar offices have been held in various countries of Europe. The holding of such offices is for example, not at all uncommon in modern France. On the Island of Malta today two of the seventeen senators are appointed by the bishop of the Diocese of Malta. The Church with utmost prudence has adapted itself as regards political matters to circumstances of time and place.[14]

A decision of the Pontifical Commission for the authentic interpretation of the Code, 1922, declared that cardinals, archbishops, and bishops, resident or titular, may not accept the office of senator or deputy without special permission of the Holy See, unless according to the constitution of the state they hold these offices *ex officio,* and the Holy See has in any way approved of the arrangement, and provided that they fulfill their ecclesiastical obligations through a vicar-general or in some other way.

In a second reply on the same date the Commission declared

[12] Zollmann, *American Church Law,* § 457.

[13] Bouuaert-Simenon, *Manuale,* I, 166; Vermeersch-Creusen, *Epitome,* I, n. 223, c.

[14] For an insight into the mind of the Holy See in these matters the recent discussion with the governor of the Island of Malta is most helpful—*cf.* Josephus Pasquazi, "Iura Sedis Apostolicae, Episcopatus et Cleri in quaestione melitensi"—*Apollinaris,* III (1930), 421-430.

that local ordinaries should be strict in granting permission to priests desirous of being candidates for legislative offices.[15] Ordinaries in granting permission to clerics to be candidates for public office should select a few priests of truly outstanding qualifications so as to present the Church in the best possible light.[16]

Once the permission of the Holy See or of the ordinary has been granted a cleric must conform himself to the principles enunciated by the Holy See both in presenting his candidacy to the electorate and in his conduct once he is elected to the office sought. This has been expressly stated by the Congregation of the Council and ordered published by the Supreme Pontiff. Once a warning on the subject has gone unheeded the cleric should be punished according to relevant canons.[17]

Third Plenary Council of Baltimore

In as far as it affects clerics soliciting and accepting legislative offices, the law of the Third Plenary Council of Baltimore against clerics interfering in purely political matters is, in substance, no greater a restriction than that of Canon 139, § 4.[18] The ordinary of the place can dispense from a law of a plenary council in a particular case and for a just cause.[19] Since these two conditions are required also by Canon 139, § 4, the law of the Code and that of the Baltimore Council on this particular point are identical, at least

[15] 25 apr., 1922—*AAS,* XIV (1922), 313.

[16] *Cf.* Heiner, "Ausschluss der Geistlichen von den politischen Wahlen"—*Archiv für katholisches Kirchenrecht,* LXXXIV (1904), 107-116; Wernz, *Ius Decretalium,* II, 225, nota 128.

[17] S. C. C., *Romana et Aliarum,* 15 mar., 1927—*AAS,* XIX (1927), 138. An anonymous article published under the title of "Dubia" in the *Jus Pontificium,* VII (1927), 10, expresses wonder that such an evident question should have been proposed. All the faithful must conform themselves to the instructions of the Holy See and the clergy should excel in so doing. The writer suggests that perhaps the question was proposed because nothing definite is found in the legislation on the obligations of clerics and, since it involves a restriction of liberty, it was deemed better and opportune to have a clear expression from the Holy See.

[18] *Cf. Concilii Plenarii Baltimorensis Tertii, Acta et Decreta,* n. 83.

[19] Canons 82 and 291, § 2.

in effect. This opinion is further strengthened by the reply of the Pontifical Commission for the Authentic Interpretation of the Code that ordinaries should be strict rather than lenient in granting permission to priests desirous of presenting themselves for legislative positions.[20]

Concordats

In Article 7 of the Concordat with Germany the State agreed that to assume political office a cleric must have the permission of the diocesan ordinary, which permission can always be revoked for serious reasons of ecclesiastical interest.[21] This agreement gives legal value in the eyes of the State to the canonical requirements. A similar agreement is had with the Italian government by virtue of Article 5 of the Lateran Pact, which article provides also that apostate priests and those under a censure will not be allowed offices which would bring them in immediate contact with the public.[22]

[20] 25 apr., 1922—*AAS,* XIV (1922), 313.

[21] September 10, 1933—*AAS,* XXV (1933), 389-414.

[22] Concordat with Italy, June 7, 1929—*AAS,* XXI (1929), 275-295. *Cf.* page 2 for the articles in various concordats which admit in general terms the right of the Church to make laws of this kind.

CHAPTER IX

BUSINESS OCCUPATIONS

Canon 142. Prohibentur clerici per se vel per alios negotiationem aut mercaturam exercere sive in propriam sive in aliorum utilitatem.

Mindful of the warning of St. Paul that "No man being a soldier to God entangleth himself with secular businesses," [1] the Church has from the beginning forbidden clerics to engage in commercial business or trading, *negotiatio aut mercatura.* Some authors claim that these two terms connote accidental differences, but all admit that as far as the present law is concerned a distinction between the two is of no practical moment. Hence they are treated here under the general terms of trading or commercial business.[2]

In the early law, however, the terms *mercatura* and *negotiatio* seem to refer rather to strictly commercial trading than to handicrafts. The term *negotium* as contrasted with *negotiatio* was broader and included all transactions made for the purpose of gain. The sharp practices of traders in these early days made such an occupation incompatible not only with clerical dignity but even unbecoming to the ordinary Christian. This is indicated by certain laws linking tradesmen with usurers and finds reflection in such comparatively recent authors as Reiffenstuel and Pirhing.[3]

Definition of Terms

Lucrative trading, *negotiatio quaestuosa, negotiatio turpis lucri causa,* that is, trading strictly speaking, is the buying of things with the intention of selling them unchanged for a higher price.

If the trading is concerned with money rather than with mer-

[1] 2 Timothy ii. 4.

[2] Vermeersch-Creusen, *Epitome,* I, n. 224, 1; Blat, *Commentarium,* II, 106.

[3] Reiffenstuel, lib. III, tit. 1, nn. 128, 129, 132; Pirhing, lib. III, tit. 50, § 1, n. I.

chandise it is called exchange, *cambium. Cambium* is subdivided into (a) *cambium manuale,* which is the immediate exchange of one form of money for money of another form; for example, the exchange of gold for silver; (b) *cambium locale,* which is had when the one conducting the exchange accepts money to be returned to the client in some other location; (c) *cambium temporale, seu fictum, obliquum, vel siccum,* which is based on the deception that the money to be given the client in another place is to be actually transported, in order that a charge might be made for the alleged transportation. This latter form is not found in modern society, as such fictitious transportation charges are made illicit by civil law.

If the transaction involves bonds or stocks—whether pertaining to the federal government, states, municipalities, to commercial or industrial companies—the trading is known as *negotiatio cambiaria.* This may take two forms. The first is a simple contract of sale in which the ownership of the bonds or stocks is exchanged immediately or almost so. In the second form the ownership changes at a determined future time, the price being determined by the exchange quotation at the time of settlement. If the purchaser intends to accept the ownership of the stocks or bonds at the determined time then, for the purposes of Canon Law, the transaction is equivalent to the simple contract of sale. However, an important distinction arises when the purchaser does not intend to accept the stocks or bonds— at times wheat, corn, etc., may be involved— on the day determined, but intends to reap the gain or suffer the loss of the difference in price quoted on the day of settlement and on the day of the original agreement.

The following may serve as an illustration. *A* purchases from *B* stock valued at one hundred dollars today to be delivered and paid for fifteen days hence. On the day agreed the same stock is worth one hundred and twenty dollars and, therefore, *A* must pay *B* twenty dollars additional for each share purchased. If, on the other hand, the stock is quoted at eighty-five dollars, *B* will lose and *A* will gain fifteen dollars on each share. In such a transaction there is no real contract of sale but a mere speculation or *playing of the exchange.*

If the material is purchased with the intention of changing it in some fashion by human labor, *e. g.*, if from wool cloth is woven, or if from grapes wine is made, in order to sell the changed product for gain the trading is known as artificial trading, *negotiatio artificialis seu industrialis*. Artificial trading is subdivided into strict artificial trading, which is had when the material is purchased with the intention of effecting the change by paid labor. This form is equivalent to lucrative trading. If the change is to be effected by one's own labor it is not to be considered equivalent to lucrative trading.

Domestic trading, *negotiatio oeconomica,* is the buying of goods for one's own use or the use of one's household and afterwards selling at a somewhat higher price some of the things because they are superfluous, or would spoil, or for some such proper reason. It differs from lucrative trading in that its primary end is not to make profit.

Community or political trading, *negotiatio politica,* is the purchasing of supplies for a large community such as a town or an army with the intention of selling them to individuals for a profit. This could take place, for example, if missionaries in a time of famine should purchase grain to sell to the poor.

Historical Conspectus

The prohibition against clerics in major orders engaging in commercial trading is found in the earliest collections. Gratian refers to the Apostolic Canons, to Canon 6 of the *Statuta Ecclesiae Antiqua,* and to the writings of Jerome, Augustine, Cyprian, Chrysostom, Isidore and Gregory as denouncing such a practice.[4] However, these early restrictions were not as severe as they were to become later when clerics were properly supported. The Council of Elvira, 305, forbade bishops, priests, and deacons from travelling through the provinces outside of their own jurisdiction for the purpose of trading, but if such an occupation should be necessary for their sustenance they should send a friend or some other person to act for them, and if they wished to trade they should do so within the province.[5]

[4] C. 3, D. XXII, c. 3-14, D. LXXXVIII.

[5] C. 18—Mansi, II, 9.

By the time of the Council of Chalcedon, 451, all bishops, clerics, and monks were forbidden to engage in business.[6] Canon 14 of the Second Provincial Council of Arles (circa 443), established the penalty of deposition and excommunication for one violating this precept.[7] Gelasius I, 494, threatened such clerics with privation of office [8] and this is found reiterated by many popes.[9]

The Roman emperors after Constantine reinforced the ecclesiastical laws with their decrees and all these Christian emperors repeated the many immunities granted clerics in this time.[10] In regard to trading the civil law follows the evolution of the ecclesiastical in that, for example, Constantine granted an immunity from all levies to those clerics desirous of supporting themselves through trading,[11] while later clerics were forbidden to trade throughout the empire.[12]

During the Middle Ages the councils frequently deplored this occupation. The Council of Tarragona, 516, in Canon 2, gives the essential definition of trading as is found in most authors, that is, the buying of things at a lower price with the intention of selling at a higher.[13]

The Council of Trent refers to the frequent sanctions in regard to this prohibition and declares that the ordinaries are to inflict the same or even greater punishments, according to their prudent judg-

[6] C. 3—Mansi, VI, 1226; VII, 394—c. 26, D. LXXXVI.

[7] Mansi, VII, 880.

[8] C. 2, D. LXXXVIII; c. 1, C. XIV, q. 4.

[9] Alexander III: c. 6, X, *ne clerici vel monachi saecularibus negotiis se immisceant,* III, 50; Coelestinus III: c. 15, X, *de electione et electi potestate,* I, 6; Innocent III and Honorius III: c. 15, 16, X, *de vita et honestate clericorum,* III, 1.

[10] Theodosian Code, XVI, 2, passim.

[11] Theodosian Code, XVI, 2, 8 and 10.

[12] Emperor Leo, Constitution LXXXVI.

[13] C. 3, C. XIV, q. 4—Mansi, VIII, 541. The following councils enacted legislation on the subject: Council of Orléans (538), c. 27—Mansi, IX, 18, 19; Council of Friuli (791), c. 5—Mansi, XIII, 847; Council of Mayence (813), c. 14—Mansi, XIV, 69; Council of Rome (826), c. 12—Mansi, XIV, 1004; Council of London (1175), c. 10—Mansi, XXII, 150; Fourth Lateran Council (1215), c. 16—Mansi, XXII, 1003, 1004; Council of Cologne (1260), c. 2—Mansi, XXIII, 1014, 1015; Council of Arles (1275), c. 14, 15—Mansi, XXIV, 151.

ment, than those prescribed in these old laws. If this prohibition had fallen into desuetude or if contrary customs had arisen, they were to give way to the strict penalties of the law, the execution of which could not be suspended by an appeal.[14]

SPECIAL PROHIBITION FOR MISSIONARIES

With the opening of the vast mission fields in the Americas and the Orient temptations arose for the missionaries to procure their sustenance and funds to carry on their work through engaging in various sorts of profitable enterprises. Against such a tendency the Supreme Pontiffs legislated forcibly. Urban VIII, 1633, referring to the consistent legislation of past centuries in a letter directed to the oriental missions, forbade all ecclesiastics, secular and religious, without exception, to engage in business pursuits whether through themselves or through others, whether in their own name or in the name of their community, whether directly or indirectly, and no matter under whatever cause or pretext. He sanctioned his law with an excommunication *ipso facto,* the deprivation of, and the impossibility in the future of attaining to, an active and passive voice in the community, the loss of all offices, ranks and dignities. Moreover the merchandise, with whatever gain acquired, was to be turned over to the use of the mission. Superiors were ordered under the same punishments to watch for such abuses and to punish the delinquents, and were deprived of the faculty of condoning such offenders or of allowing them to retain some part of the said merchandise or gain therefrom.[15]

This legislation of Urban VIII is cited in such detail, for it is contained in the legislation of the Code today; the penalties, however, are much milder.[16]

An important concession was granted in this matter by the Congregation for the Propagation of the Faith under date of November 23, 1665, but there was a particular reason present. The Holy

[14] Conc. Trident., Sess. XXII, *de ref.*, c. 1.

[15] Urbanus VIII, litt. ap. "*Ex debito,*" 22 febr., 1633, § 8—*Fontes,* n. 211.

[16] *Cf.* Canons 2379, 2380.

Father had granted permission to a certain vicar apostolic to ordain candidates, even to the priesthood, without the necessary patrimony. So it was asked if such clerics—in view of the fact that there were no other means to provide for their sustenance—could engage in business pursuits, to invest their money with merchants, and to form business concerns with them. The response permitted the toleration of this practice with the proviso that the contracts entered into be intrinsically licit and that no more should be invested than what constituted a legitimate patrimony.[17]

Clement IX a short time later, 1669, found it necessary to restate the legislation of Urban VIII, because under a variety of subterfuges missionaries were ignoring the law. This new legislation differed little from that of Urban. It did provide, however, that a violating of the law even on one occasion was sufficient to incur the penalties; the merchandise and gain therefrom were not to be turned over to the religious society to which the delinquent belonged but were to be used for charitable purposes by the representatives of the Holy See. Superiors were held by the same penalties, if they did not punish, at least by removal, a cleric offending in any way in this matter. The excommunication *ipso facto* incurred by such delinquents could not be absolved outside of the danger of death by anyone, no matter what his faculties, unless the gain be turned over to the proper authorities.[18]

The excommunication *ipso facto* resulting from a violation of these laws was declared to be in force even as late as 1872.[19] Eleven years later the Holy Office declared that, even though Clement's legislation did not mention China, still that country was included, but that the censure should be changed to one reserved simply to the Supreme Pontiff. A declaratory interpretation stated that Clement's legislation affected not only European missionaries, but all ecclesiastics who under the name of missionaries or under any other title were sent to those regions or stayed there for any length of time.[20]

[17] S. C. de Prop. Fide, 23 nov., 1665, ad I—*Fontes*, n. 4473.

[18] Clemens IX, const. "*Solicitudo,*" 17 iunii, 1669—*Fontes*, n. 243.

[19] S. C. S. Off., 4 dec., 1872—*Fontes*, n. 1023.

[20] S. C. S. Off., 17 ian., 1883—*Fontes*, n. 1077.

Legislation for the Universal Church

To return to the chronological development, Benedict XIV complained that in spite of past legislation clerics were still engaging in business affairs under the names of others. One of the first acts of his pontificate was to put an end to the opinion held by some authors that trading could be done through the agency of another. As stated above, Urban VIII and Clement IX had enacted such a prohibition for missionary lands and a similar provision appears in some of the earlier councils—such as Orléans in the year 538—quoted above on page 69.

Benedict therefore repeated the laws of his predecessors and made the additional statement that the fact that an established business was inherited by a cleric did not free him from the necessity of giving it up, nor could he escape such duty even though he held it conjointly with other goods and other heirs, and even though the inheritance be administered under the name of a lay person. However if such a business could not be disposed of immediately without temporal loss to the cleric, he should, if he lived within Italy or the adjacent islands, obtain permission from the Congregation of the Council to retain it for a time under the administration of a layman; if he lived in other regions he should obtain permission from the same Congregation or from the ordinary of the place. If the cleric should act without such permission, or should ignore one of the above provisions, he would incur all of the penalties.[21]

Clement XIII renewed verbatim the preceding legislation and condemned as an abuse and a corruption of the law any contrary custom. He expressly warned superiors not to allow themselves to be deceived by the pretexts and apparently good intentions of their subjects. If any doubts should arise as to the licitness of these contracts the case should be sent to the Congregation of the Council for decision. Exchanges and bourses, *cambium activum,* were to be considered as a species of business. A cleric excusing himself from faults in this matter, not because of his own necessity, but because of the needs of others to whom he was bound by natural ties, is to be subjected to the penalties unless he at least exposed the case and

[21] Benedictus XIV, const. "*Apostolicae servitutis,*" 25 febr., 1741, pars. 1, 2—*Fontes*, n. 306; *cf.* also Benedict XIV, *De Synodo Dioecesana*, X, 6, 5.

requested the permission of the Holy See, if living within Italy and the adjacent islands, or of the ordinary of the place, if residing in remoter regions.[22]

Further Legislation Applying to Missionaries

The Holy Office in 1782 issued an instruction, on orders of the Holy Father, in answer to the query as to whether priests ordained for the missions without benefice or patrimony and lacking sufficient Mass stipends could invest money in business enterprises, and accept part of the profit for their sustenance. A distinction was made between those clerics who at the time were without sustenance and in detriment to their sacredotal character forced to beg for a livelihood, and those clerics who foreseeing such future needs were desirous of making provision for these needs. For the first group reference was made to the decree of the Sacred Congregation of the Propaganda, 1665, quoted above, while for the second group the encyclical of Clement XIII, "*Cum primum,*" cited in the above paragraph was to be applied.[23]

The Sacred Congregation for the Propagation of the Faith answered several queries concerning the converting of money destined for the missions into merchandise or into objects made of coral to be resold as the needs of the missionaries demanded. The reasons alleged for the requests were that in some places money was not in use, or, if in use, was estimated by the natives as of little value while the coral objects, for example, could be sold even for gain. It was also stated that having the money in merchandise lessened the danger of possible robberies at the hands of pirates or carriers and attendants, and likewise avoided the excessive taxes of the government.

Uniformly the congregation responded that such practices were allowed but that the goods or coral objects bought with the money should be exchanged directly through barter for the necessities of life and in this way only.[24]

[22] Clemens XIII, ep. encycl. "*Cum primum,*" 17 sept., 1759, pars. 4-10—*Fontes,* n. 452.

[23] S. C. S. Off. (*Constantinop.*), 18 mart., 1782—*Fontes,* n. 845; *cf.* also S. C. S. Off. instr. (*ad Vic. Ap. Constantinop.*), 18 mart., 1784, ad 8—*Fontes,* n. 847.

[24] S. C. de Prop. Fide, instr. (*C. P. pro Sin.*), 13 ian., 1665, ad I—*Collectanea* (ed. 1907), n. 160; S. C. S. Off., 6 mart., 1777—*Collectanea* (ed. 1907), n. 520.

Permission in a later century was granted to sell for money the merchandise sent the missions for their support.[25] However the Sacred Congregation seemed loath to grant permission beyond exchanging the goods through barter to supply the necessities of life and seemed desirous that each case be presented to the congregation. At the same time the congregation warned the missionaries to abstain from all study and planning for gain, and if any profit should result it should be applied to the mission and not to the individual missionary, and such permissions were not to be viewed as allowing missionaries to engage in trading in order to devote the profit to the mission.[26] Missionaries were not allowed to enter into partnerships with merchants and to accept the gain from their trading.[27]

Another difficulty arose in those places where mission activities were forbidden by the rulers under severe punishments and where all foreigners were forbidden to enter unless they paid a high price for the privilege of trading among the natives. In order to approach these peoples the missionaries were allowed to carry on trading, provided that it was done through another person and that nothing be done which would condone superstition. The same response allowed a vicar apostolic to own his own boat for the purpose of transporting students to and from Europe and to attend to other needs of the mission. In order to avoid the suspicion of the natives and to cover the cost of the voyages, merchandise could be bought and sold, that is, as above stated through a third person.[28]

Perhaps it was through a misinterpretation of such faculties as the above that a vicar apostolic, in allowing missionaries to trade in certain regions of Thibet incurred the great displeasure of the Sacred Congregation of the Propaganda and provoked a condemnation couched in the strongest language. All foreigners, particularly Euro-

[25] S. C. de Prop. Fide, instr. (*C. P. pro Sin.*), 13 aug., 1834—*Collectanea* (ed. 1907), n. 836; S. C. S. Off. (*Coreae*), 12 febr., 1851, ad 6—*Fontes*, n. 915.

26 S. C. de Prop. Fide, instr. (*C. P. pro Sin.*), 10 ian., 1837—*Collectanea* (ed. 1893), n. 344; S. C. de Prop. Fide, instr. (*ad Vic. Ap. Tunk. Occid.*), 10 aug., 1841—*Collectanea* (ed. 1893), n. 345.

[27] S. C. S. Off., 29 ian., 1851—*Collectanea* (ed. 1907), n. 1056.

[28] S. C. de Prop. Fide—*Ex. aud. SSmi.*, 20 aug., 1849—*Collectanea* (ed. 1907), n. 1037.

peans, were forbidden under penalty of expulsion, to enter into certain regions of Thibet, except for the purpose of trading. So the vicar apostolic, judging that there was no other way to convert the people from idolatry, allowed missionaries to set up a regular business concern with stores located at strategic points for the purpose of selling goods. After a time the vicar apostolic informed the Holy See of the practice and was immediately ordered in the strongest terms to terminate such activity and furthermore was threatened with grave punishments if he did not do so immediately. The congregation stated that certain privileges in this regard had been granted in particular cases, but never had missionaries been allowed to engage in lucrative trading precisely as a means of propagating the Catholic faith. Such a practice would earn the contempt of the pagans. Missionaries skilled in medicine could distribute prescriptions gratuitously or at least without gain; for the rest they would have to strive to evangelize those who attended the hospital or mission schools.[29]

Certain difficulties arising with the introduction of foreign priests in America to provide for the large number of immigrants during the last fifty years or so provoked a letter of instruction from the Sacred Congregation of the Council addressed to the bishops of America and Italy, which required that the bishops have moral certitude that these priests would not stain the dignity of the priesthood by engaging in any common occupation not in keeping with their status.[30] The same congregation in 1903 issued a general law on the same subject. The ordinaries of America and Italy were to be held to the strict observance of the former declaration Similar provisions were made affecting priests who intended to take up the ministry in the Philippine Islands.[31]

Discipline of the Code

Since Canon 142 contains the identical legislation, couched in practically the same words as the old law, the discipline of the Code is to be interpreted in accordance with pre-Code legislation, and the

29 S. C. de Prop. Fide—litt. (*ad Vic. Ap. Lahassae*), 4 febr., 1860—*Collectanea* (ed. 1907), n. 1184; *cf.* etiam S. C. de Prop. Fide, litt. (*ad Vic. Ap. Lahassae*), 8 apr., 1862—*Collectanea* (ed. 1893), n. 350.

30 S. C. C., litt. encycl., 27 iul., 1890, n. 3—*Fontes*, n. 4280.

31 S. C. C., 14 nov., 1903, nn. I, II, III—*Fontes*, n. 4315.

interpretations already given by approved authors treating of the old discipline are to be followed.[32] Summarily therefore the legislation of Canon 142 may be stated as follows: Clerics, religious and those living in imitation of religious in conformity with Canon 679, § 1, cannot lawfully exercise lucrative commercial trading, or artificial trading if the goods be changed through hired labor, whether the enterprise be conducted through themselves or through others, whether for their own utility or for the utility of others, unless they have been granted permission by proper ecclesiastical authority or unless they are faced with grave necessity affecting their own sustenance or that of those to whom they are obligated.[33]

Reasons Underlying This Prohibition

Throughout the past legislation, popes, councils and canonists have expressed in varying ways the purpose of the law of Canon 142. These motives may be summed up as follows: (1) Trading involves innumerable cares which lead to a neglect of and a distraction from the duties connected with the clerical and religious state. (2) There is the danger of absorbing a spirit of cupidity and avarice with its consequent vices. (3) There arises the peril that clerics and religious might become involved in civil suits. (4) There is always present the possibility that such enterprises may result in fraud, damages, perjury, etc. (5) From a cleric's engagement in such occupations there arises the likelihood of a serious lessening of the people's esteem of the sacred ministry. This latter reason was urged more forcibly in regard to missionaries, for the pagans were inclined to believe that Europeans were interested only in the exploitation of their lands and goods.[34]

As Benedict XIV pointed out, the fact that the trading is carried

[32] Canon 6, 2°; *cf.* also Vermeersch-Creusen, *Epitome,* I, n. 224.

[33] *Cf.* Vromant, *De Negotiatione Clericis et Religiosis Interdicta,* n. 20; Vermeersch-Creusen, *Epitome,* I, n. 224; for a full treatment of the inclusion of religious and those living in imitation of religious in conformity with Canon 673, § 1, the reader is referred to pages 2-3 of this dissertation.

[34] *Cf.* Clemens XIII, ep. encycl., *"Cum primum,"* 17 sept., 1759—*Fontes,* n. 452; Schmalzgrueber, lib. III, tit. 50, n. 6; Vermeersch-Creusen, *Epitome,* I, n. 224, 2.

on by means of an agent does not make the cleric less anxious and solicitious for gain. He based this statement on experience.[35] A Coronata would include commercial trading among those occupations which are so completely foreign to the clerical state as to seem to be always repugnant to clerics and which can become licit only in extraordinary cases.[36] Benedict XIV quotes two authorities who held the opinion that the legislation—which is now repeated in Canon 142—is based on divine law, but such an opinion, to say the least, seems far-fetched, especially in view of the instances of bishops and clerics engaging in trading, as illustrated on the following page.[37]

Strictly Commercial Trading

As stated above, strictly commercial trading, *negotiatio lucrativa seu quaestuosa,* is defined as the buying of things with the intention of selling them unchanged at a higher price. To constitute trading in the strict sense, therefore, four elements are required: (1) That the object be bought. (2) That it be bought precisely with the intention of selling it. (3) That the article be left unchanged. (4) That it be sold at a higher price. If any one of these elements be missing, then trading in the strict sense is not present. It is essential to bear this fact in mind always and so to avoid the grouping of all occupations for gain under the prohibition of Canon 142. As Schmalzgrueber points out, some forget this distinction and confuse *negotiatio* with *negotium,* since both are done for gain.[38] *Negotium* is broader and includes all forms of gainful occupations.

Artificial Trading

In addition to strict commercial trading the Church has condemned strict artificial trading—*negotiatio artificialis seu industrialis*— which may be defined as the buying of material with the intention of changing it by means of *hired* labor and of selling the article at

[35] Benedictus XIV, const., *"Apostolicae Servitutis,"* 25 febr., 1741—*Fontes,* n. 306.

[36] A Coronata, *Institutiones,* I, n. 200.

[37] Benedict XIV, *De Synodo Dioecesana,* X, 6, 1.

[38] Schmalzgrueber, lib. III, tit. 50, n. 7.

a profit. If the change be effected by the cleric's own labor he merits no condemnation. However, when paid labor is used the trading approximates strictly commercial trading and is prohibited, since both the material and the labor are bought. This has been the constant opinion of the Holy See and of Canonists.[39]

It is primarily against commercial trading and strict artificial trading that the legislation of the Church has been directed throughout the centuries. If in imitation of St. Paul a cleric bought material with the intention of changing it by his own labor and then selling it at the current market price in order to provide for his own sustenance, or for those dependent upon him, or for the poor—without, of course, neglecting his duties—he was not condemned, but rather commended for so doing.[40] Benedict XIV quotes various sources as establishing the fact that many bishops and priests in imitation of St. Paul took up labors which were neither against the dignity of their state nor hindered their care of souls. They undertook such labors for their own sustenance and for that of the poor.[41]

Domestic Trading

Domestic trading, *negotiatio oeconomica,* is the buying of goods for one's own use, or for the use of one's household or community, and the subsequent selling of the same goods or of some portion of them at a price somewhat higher, in as far as they have proven superfluous, or because they would spoil or for some like proper reason. It differs from lucrative trading in that its primary end is not the making of profit, but the prudent administration of one's possessions. Hence, it is not only permissible, but at times even mandatory.[42] This has been the recognized discipline of the Church.

There are, however, certain restrictions placed on the exercise of domestic trading. It must be done in a way that harmonizes with the dignity and decorum of the clerical state, and not in the

[39] *Cf.* Lingen et Reuss, *Causae Selectae S. C. C.*, nn. 119-122; Schmalzgrueber, lib. III, tit. 50, n. 18.

[40] *Cf.* cc. 3, 4, D. XCI.

[41] Benedict XIV, *De Synodo Dioecesana,* X, 6, 2.

[42] *Cf.* Canons 1522 to 1524.

fashion of traders. It must not involve scandal, nor give rise to any suspicion of fraud, nor result in the neglect of the cleric's duties and obligations. A cleric or superior cannot, of course, hide real commercial trading under the guise of domestic trading by buying more than the community could possibly use.[43]

Domestic administration does not divert the cleric from the duties or obligations of his state nor does it implicate him in secular occupations. If such sane administration of one's goods were forbidden to clerics and religious they would suffer grave loss.[44]

The goods may be sold at a higher price of course. If they were not sold higher than the purchase price there would be no question of trading in the accepted meaning of the word. It seems also that the articles can be sold even if they are not really superfluous and even though the seller has the intention of later buying similar goods, since they were not originally purchased for the purpose of gain.[45] This should not be done constantly, however, as such a practice mighty frustrate the purpose of the law.

Community Trading

Community trading, *negotiatio politica,* is the purchasing of supplies for a large community, such as a town or an army, with the intention of selling them to individuals for profit. Some authors fail to bear in mind that, if this is not done at a profit, then it ceases to be trading in the accepted meaning of the term, although it might fall under the general prohibition of Canon 139, § 1, as being foreign to the clerical state. This is the contention of Maroto, Blat and Ayrinhac.[46]

All canonists maintain that ordinarily and *per se* community trading is forbidden. Chelodi and Cappello, moreover, state that it is forbidden even though it be done for a religious, charitable or social

[43] Wernz, *Ius Decretalium,* II, n. 219; Cappello, *Summa Iuris Canonici,* I, n. 247, 5; A Coronata, *Institutiones,* I, n. 200.

[44] Wernz-Vidal, *De Personis,* n. 128.

[45] Schmalzgrueber, lib. III, tit. 50, n. 10; Vromant, *De Negotiatione,* n. 27.

[46] Maroto, *Institutiones,* n. 572, II, B; Blat, *Commentarium,* II, 106; Ayrinhac, *General Legislation,* p. 312.

end.[47] A Coronata, in maintaining that community trading is prohibited in view of the hazards attendant upon the administration of the funds involved, nevertheless leaves room for an exception in the the case of necessity, of mercy, or of charity. Judgment relative to the merit of these claims pertains, as he says, to the ordinary.[48] Schmalzgrueber admits an exception in case of grave interest to the country or to the common good.[49] Vromant asserts that community trading is not forbidden if the intention is only to supply the necessities of some community, although the articles be sold at a price sufficient to include the costs of transportation, wages of helpers, etc.[50] Vermeersch-Creusen state that the licitness of domestic trading is to be judged from the manner and end. If the end is not to acquire gain and if it is conducted in a way not foreign to the clerical state, they say that it does not seem to be prohibited. It is, they conclude, not forbidden to clerics to sell books, etc., to students, or to offer for sale pictures, statues, rosaries, etc., in some place of pilgrimage. A moderate profit is allowed to care for the expense of transportation, and a small remuneration for the one in charge, etc. Sedulously all forms of common profit-making must be avoided.[51]

The position of Chelodi and Cappello, who maintain that community trading is forbidden even for religious, charitable or social aims, is explained by the likelihood that they are considering normal conditions and not such extraordinary situations as a famine, etc. In other words, they maintain simply that it is not licit to exercise community trading for the purpose of applying the profit to the poor, or of acquiring the financial means to assist missionaries in spreading the gospel, or for the betterment of social standards. If this be their opinion, then it is identical with that of the other authors. It is true that in normal times community trading even for such ends is forbidden, as is made evident throughout the legislation of the Church.

It would seem that in times of famine and similar disasters it

[47] Chelodi, *Ius de Personis,* p. 212; Cappello, *Summa Iuris Canonici,* I, n. 248, 1, 3.

[48] A Coronata, *Institutiones,* I, n. 200.

[49] Schmalzgrueber, lib. III, tit. 50, nn. 13, 14.

[50] Vromant, *Ius Missionariorum,* II: *De Personis,* n. 411.

[51] Vermeersch-Creusen, *Epitome,* I, n. 224, 2.

would be foreign to Christian charity to make a profit from community trading. But once the profit element is removed, then the transactions of trading cease to come under the prohibition of Canon 142. An increase in price for transportation and labor items certainly does not constitute profit and hence is not prohibited. However the modern concept of economists that a just salary—in this case to accrue to the benefit of some cleric—is to be included in the costs of operations, and therefore not to be considered as profit, cannot be applied here.

To summarize, community trading is forbidden ordinarily and *per se*. In times of disaster it may and frequently should be applied in a way becoming to clerics and without any appearance of profit, and hence not trading in the real meaning of the term. In normal times the opinion of Vermeersch-Creusen in regard to the sale of religious articles in some place of pilgrimage—with the precautions they apply—seems feasible for practice. A further consideration of the sale of religious articles is found below on pages 84 and 85.

Money Exchange

Clerics are forbidden to engage either through themselves or through others in the exchange of money for profit, whether this exchange takes on the form of *cambium manuale, locale,* or *temporale*.[52] An explicit prohibition is found in the constitutions of Benedict XIV and Clement XIII, and in a number of Rota decisions.[53]

Trading in Mass Stipends

The Code contains in Canons 827, 828, and 840, § 1, a special prohibition against even the semblance of trading in Mass stipends. Canon 2324 states that such a delict is to be punished by the ordinary according to the gravity of the crime, not excluding, if war-

[52] A definition of terms is found on pages 66 and 67.

[53] Benedictus XIV, const. "*Apostolicae servitutis*," 25 febr., 1741—*Fontes*, n. 306; Clemens XIII, ep. encycl. "*Cum primum*," 17 sept., 1759—*Fontes*, n. 452; *cf.* also *Sacrae Romanae Rotae Decisiones Recentiores*, decisio 173, n. 6, partis 14 and decisio 251, n. 5 et n. 6, partis 14; *cf.* also Benedict XIV, *De Synodo Diocesana*, X, 6, 4.

ranted, suspension or privation of benefice or of ecclesiastical office, or, if a layman be involved, excommunication. This legislation is not treated here *ex professo*.[54]

Activities Not Forbidden to Clerics

The writing and selling of one's own books for profit is a species of artificial trading not forbidden to clerics. This has been expressly decided by the Holy Office In the same response it was declared that generally speaking clerics are not allowed to sell books written or edited by others, even though they intend to devote the proceeds to charity, but in particular cases the ordinary should be consulted and his judgment followed. [55]

A cleric may buy a block of valuable wood in order to carve from it a statue which he intends to sell later at a rather high price with profit.[56] He may also buy goods, change them through his own labor and sell them at the current price, if he does this not for a mere desire for gain but for some honest and laudable purpose. The reason is that the goods are sold in a changed condition which has been effected, not by the price of employed labor, but by the laudable efforts of personal enterprise, and the purpose of the trading is not for the sake of profit. Therefore, in imitation of St. Paul and the early monks, clerics may—in agreement with the interpretation of Schmalzgrueber and others—make nets, baskets, rugs, tents, etc., in order to provide for themselves, to avoid idleness, to mortify the body, to give alms, or for other similar reasons, and then sell the articles at a time when free from the performance of specific spiritual duties.[57]

It is licit to buy animals, let them graze on one's own fields, and then sell them for gain at the current price, or to secure profit from their offspring, wool, milk, etc.[58] However it would seem that

[54] *Cf.* Keller, Charles Frederick, *Mass Stipends*; Catholic University of America: Washington, 1925.

[55] S. C. S. Off., 10 iun., 1846—*Fontes,* n. 897.

[56] Wernz-Vidal, *De Personis,* n. 2. 128, III.

[57] Schmalzgrueber, lib. III, tit. 50, n. 19.

[58] Vromant, *Ius Missionariorum,* II: *De Personis,* n. 417; Schmalzgrueber, lib. III, tit. 50, n. 17,—who quotes a decision of the Sacred Congregation of the Council; St. Alphonsus, *Theologia Moralis,* III, n. 835.

some restriction is to be placed upon the number of animals that may be so purchased. In one particular instance the Sacred Congregation of Bishops and Regulars—although admitting that it is permissible to buy animals to consume the grasses of one's own fields or of the fields of the community for which a cleric or clerics contribute a share, or when the offspring of the animals serve for one's own use and not for gain—allowed a community to retain at a maximum a hundred such animals.[59]

The selling of Christmas cards and similar compositions of a religious nature, if designed and printed under the supervision of clerics, to secure funds for religious and charitable purposes, seems licit.

Religious are also allowed to conduct laundries in conjunction with the management of a reform school for girls.

It is licit for clerics to sell the articles made by students of trade schools for a profit in order to support teachers, even though a small sum be paid the students as a compensation for their labor. In this case no offense is given to the public and the labor is not fully compensated, and profit is not the primary motive.[60]

If a friend should sell a cleric an object at a bargain, the latter could resell it for a just price, because the gain comes from a free donation. Of course it is not licit if the low price results from a wholesale purchase of articles which the cleric intends to sell at retail.[61] Nor would a cleric be justified in searching for bargain prices with the intention of selling the articles thus purchased for profit at their usual market value.

It is not forbidden for clerics to have hired workers make articles from the goods of benefices, patrimonies, or from their own goods not purchased for that express purpose, all of which is done merely that

[59] S. C. Ep. and Reg., *Cisterciensium Montis Soractis,* 17 aug., 1792—*Fontes,* n. 1886; *cf.* etiam Bizzari, *Collectanea ad usum secretariae S. C. Ep. et Reg.,* p. 399.

[60] Vermeersch-Creusen, *Epitome,* I, n. 224, 2; Vromant, *De Negotiatione,* n. 24; Cappello, *Summa Iuris Canonici,* I, n. 248, 1, 2; A Coronata, *Institutiones,* I, n. 200, nota 6.

[61] Vromant, *Ius Missionariorum,* II: *De Personis,* n. 418, 7; also Vromant, *De Negotiatione,* n. 27.

the goods might find a readier market. Thus, for instance, it is permissible to have paid labor to make wine from their own grapes and to sell the wine at a profit.[62]

Clerics may also buy materials from which workers hired by themselves make garments and similar articles, not indeed for gain, but for their own use.[63]

Clerics may loan money to traders as to other persons.[64] This gives them no part in the business.

It seems licit for a cleric to conduct a photographic studio in his house to take pictures of clients for a moderate profit, especially if the cleric has need of sustenance. This is clearly not prohibited trading and does not seem unbecoming. However the same could not be done in a public establishment or office, nor with neglect of duty, nor in any way that proved unbecoming to the clerical state.[65] It would be preferable, nevertheless, to consult the ordinary in this matter.

It seems licit also for a monastery to purchase a field with a ripe harvest and to sell whatever is superfluous. The primary object is the purchase of the field and it is only accidental that the harvest is ready to be gathered. In reality the transaction is the same as selling the fruits of one's own fields.[66]

In reselling an article it is permissible to make charges for the expenses of transportation, storage, conservation, etc., for these are considered part of the cost and do not constitute any real gain.[67]

The fact that the objects traded are of a religious nature does not make the trading licit. Clerics, therefore, are not justified in establishing agencies or shops for the purpose of selling religious vestments, candles, sacred appurtenances, religious books, rosaries, etc.,

[62] Wernz, *Ius Decretalium,* II, n. 219, III; A Coronata, *Institutiones,* I, n. 200.

[63] De Meester, *Compendium,* I, n. 387, b.

[64] Blat, *Commentarium,* II, 106.

[65] "Se un sacerdote puo esercitare l'arte fotografica," *Il Monitore Ecclesiastico,* XXV (1913-1914), 419, 420.

[66] Schmalzgrueber, lib. III, tit. 50, n. 19, cum Molina contra Lassarte.

[67] Vromant, *De Negotiatione,* n. 27; also Vromant, *Ius Missionariorum,* II: *De Personis,* n. 418, 8.

in order to procure profit thereby.[68] However it is licit, as a convenience to the faithful, to sell objects of small moment, such as crosses, rosaries, pictures, books, etc., in some place of pilgrimage or to visitors at some religious establishment. This, however, should not be done for profit, although a price may be asked which will compensate for the expenses incident to the purchase, transportation, etc. If a layman is employed in connection with their sale a small compensation may be made also for his services. All appearances, however, of common profit-making must be sedulously avoided.[69]

All authors admit that it is licit to cultivate one's own fields with the aid of hired labor and to sell the harvest for profit.

It is licit to rent to another one's own fields or animals for profit.[70] However it does not seem licit to purchase animals with the precise intention of hiring them out for a fee, although they may be hired out occasionally. This is the common opinion.[71] De Lugo maintained that the purchase of animals with the intention of hiring them out was licit *per se*, but said that some species of trading was present if more and more animals should be bought for this purpose.[72]

It seems illicit to purchase or rent land for raising wheat, corn, etc., or for the grazing of animals, with the sole purpose of selling the products or animals for a gain.[73] Vromant expresses the follow-

[68] Pistocchi, *I Canoni Penali*, p. 293, nota 1; Mothon, *Institutions Canoniques*, I, n. 251; Schäfer, *De Religiosis*, p. 512.

[69] Schäfer, *De Religiosis*, p. 512; Vermeersch-Creusen, *Epitome*, I, n. 224, 2; De Meester, *Compendium*, I, n. 387. De Meester remarks that it is preferable to have a layman own and operate such affairs lest under the veil of serving the people there be hidden a desire for gain, or lest the cleric be the object of suspicion.

[70] Reiffenstuel, lib. III, tit. 1, n. 135; Schmalzgrueber—lib. III, tit. 50, n. 17—adduces a decision of the Sacred Congregation of the Council; Aertnys-Damen, *Theologia Moralis*, I, n. 1138. This is admitted by all authors.

[71] Schmalzgrueber, lib. III, tit. 50, n. 17; Vromant, *De Negotiatione*, n. 26; Ballerini-Palmieri, *Opus Theologicum Morale*, n. 467.

[72] De Lugo, *De Iustitia et Iure*, disp. 26, n. 34.

[73] Augustine, *Commentary*, II, 96; Aertnys-Damen, *Theologia Moralis*, I, n. 1138; Cocchi, *Commentarium*, II, 141; De Meester, *Compendium*, I, n. 387, b; Barbosa, *Tractatus Varii*, p. 262; St. Alphonsus, *Theologia Moralis*, III, nn. 834, 835. The latter considers this teaching confirmed by the third canon of the Council of Chalcedon—c. 1, C. XXI, q. 3.

ing opinion: Authors assert that clerics are forbidden to rent fields for feeding flocks or for the purpose of selling fruits raised in such fields. But, since in view of Canon 1541 the contract of renting is no longer to be compared to a contract of sale, this is sometimes not strictly trading: *e.g.*, if a cleric having a field rents another as a supplement or as a means of avoiding inconveniences caused by troublesome neighbors.[74] It is commonly admitted that clerics are allowed to rent an adjacent field as a supplement to take care of a growing flock or to avoid bothersome neighbors, but this is allowed because the primary aim is not for profit but for some other cause.[75] To say that the Code does not consider the contract of renting equivalent to the contract of sale,[76] is to beg the question. Canon 1541 refers rather to the solemnities to be observed and does not affect the nature of the contract. Admittedly before the Code the nature of these two contracts differed essentially in canonical legislation and, as St. Alphonsus points out, the element of renting took the transaction out of the strict realm of trading, but it nevertheless was expressly forbidden by the Council of Chalcedon prohibiting clerics to rent the fields of another for the purpose of gain.[77] St. Alphonsus admits, however, the possibility of a contrary custom, as does Bastien.[78]

It appears licit for clerics to feed their own flocks with produce bought from another. This is not strictly speaking trading and the profit in selling the animals comes rather from the labor of their care. Such care, too, has not been considered unbecoming to the clerical state and as a rule no scandal will be present. As long as the obligation is doubtful it does not bind.[79]

[74] Vromant, *De Negotiatione*, n. 25; also in *Ius Missionariorum*, II: *De Personis*, n. 417.

[75] De Meester, *Compendium*, I, n. 387, b; Schmalzgrueber, lib. III, tit. 50, n. 17.

[76] Cocchi (*Commentarium*, II, 141) says that the Code does consider them equivalent.

[77] St. Alphonsus, *Theologia Moralis*, III, nn. 834, 835.

[78] St. Alphonsus, *Theologia Moralis*, III, n. 835; Bastien, *Directoire Canonique*, n. 518.

[79] This is the opinion of St. Alphonsus, *Theologia Moralis*, III, n. 835, who, however, quotes opposing opinions.

As stated above, artificial or industrial trading is prohibited. The decretalists taught this opinion, but hesitated to bring such trading strictly under this prohibition. Pirhing, for example, and Schmalzgrueber considered it forbidden as being unbecoming to the clerical state.[80] Blat seems to be influenced by them in calling this form of trading *quaedam negotiatio palliata*. He says that it is not trading properly speaking. Therefore, he concludes, it is not forbidden by virtue of Canon 142, but falls under the general clauses of either Canon 138 or Canon 139, § 1.[81] Now, however, the terminology is clearer and the majority of modern authors say that artificial trading is forbidden by Canon 142. It is forbidden, therefore, to buy grapes, wool, iron, etc., to have paid servants make wine, cloth, iron objects, etc., to sell for profit. In this case the cleric would be buying both materials and labor and so nothing essentially is missing to constitute forbidden trading. The definition of lucrative trading embraces only that form of trading for profit when the materials are left unchanged, but if they are changed by hired labor the trading is forbidden under the name of artificial or industrial trading.

It is licit to have hired labor change the products of one's own fields and to sell them for profit. Thus it is licit to have paid labor make wine from the grapes of one's own vineyard. There is some dispute, though, as to the licitness of selling these products at retail. Augustine, following Heiner, says that it is not licit to sell wine, oil, or other products at retail.[82] Vromant expresses the same opinion as do Genicot-Salsmans.[83] Ferraris on the other hand says that it is licit to sell wine and bread made from one's own products and to sell these at retail. He quotes a decision of the Sacred Congregation of Bishops and Regulars.[84] Schmalzgrueber would allow these products to be sold at retail provided the sales are conducted

[80] Pirhing, lib. III, tit. 50, 1, n. IV; Schmalzgrueber, lib. III, tit. 50, n. 18. These authors say that it is forbidden *per epikeiam*, as does De Lugo, *De Iustitia et Iure*, disp. 26, n. 34.

[81] Blat, *Commentarium*, II, 105.

[82] Augustine, *Commentary*, II, 97, footnote 76.

[83] Vromant, *De Negotiatione*, n. 25; also Vromant, *Ius Missionariorum*, II: *De Personis*, n. 417; Genicot-Salsmans, *Theologiae Moralis Institutiones*, n. 39.

[84] Ferraris, *Prompta Bibliotheca*, "clericus," art. III, n. 15.

by others, that is, through servants or relatives. He alleges two decisions of the Holy See and states that the prohibition forbidding clerics to own inns, *cauponae,* refers to places where the wine is actually consumed on the premises. However, he states, as does Pirhing, that the wine cannot be retailed at the home of the cleric.[85]

By way of criticism it is evident that selling at retail one's own products does not constitute any forbidden form of trading. The question is rather whether such acts are unbecoming to the clerical state. This in turn depends a great deal on the customs of the times and place. The interpretation of Heiner, Augustine, Vromant and Genicot-Salsmans seems too strict to state in such general terms. However the precautions urged by Schmalzgrueber should be observed. If there is any danger of scandal the ordinary should be consulted. Of course all reasonable possibilities of selling these products at wholesale should be exhausted.

Schmalzgrueber maintains that clerics are not allowed to purchase mines in order to make a profit from the sale of the metal extracted by hired laborers.[86] Cappello likewise embraces this opinion.[87] Cocchi also favors this opinion, particularly if many workers are hired.[88] D'Annibale says that it is not illicit to purchase a mine with the intention of extracting the metal through paid labor and selling it for gain.[89] Such a transaction does seem illicit in view of the reason stated before, namely, that in this case both the product and the labor are purchased. In this case it would seem that lucrative trading strictly speaking is had, for the product itself remains unchanged and is sold at a higher price. The only change made is one of place which is only *per accidens.* However it is licit to purify salt or to extract iron, etc., from one's *own* mines, through paid labor and to sell the products for profit. If land is purchased not knowing that it contains oil, metals, etc., the extraction of these products through hired labor would be licit.[90]

85 Schmalzgrueber, lib. III, tit. 50, n. 17; Pirhing, lib. III, tit. 50, § 1, n. V.

86 Schmalzgrueber, lib. III, tit. 50, n. 18.

87 Cappello, *Summa Iuris Canonici,* I, 300, nota 13.

88 Cocchi, *Commentarium,* II, 139.

89 D'Annibale, *Summula,* III, n. 155, nota 5.

90 Schmalzgrueber, lib. III, tit. 50, n. 17.

Clerics Must Avoid Unbecoming Actions

In performing the various transactions not forbidden by Canon 142 clerics should sedulously avoid any act which might bring discredit to themselves and offer scandal to the people. The authors constantly refer to this warning. Mothon states that in many dioceses the bishops have forbidden clerics to employ, without the previous authorization of the ordinary, any sort of printed advertisement, especially in newspapers, to sell their produce, fruits, or articles made by their own industry.[91]

Although certain transactions in themselves may be licit, nevertheless clerics or a monastery, for instance, would not be justified in embarking on such large-scale production as would require, for example, the construction of a factory for the manufacture of cloth from the wool of their own sheep. Maroto agrees with this, but makes the possible exception in a case where the wool could not be conveniently sold in any other way.[92]

Such a case is not likely to arise and certainly the concession is rather broad. The ordinary's authority should certainly be secured and he would hardly be justified in giving a favorable opinion without consulting the Holy See.

A cleric should not set up a public store in which to sell the objects of his own labor as this seems unbecoming.[93] In exercising domestic trading particular care should be taken not to give scandal or suspicion of fraud or furnish occasion for hidden trading merely for the sake of gain.[94] As stated before, in order to constitute any form of trading, prohibited as such, the element of profit must be present. It would, therefore, not be trading if goods are bought and sold without profit to friends or the poor.[95] However such practices,

[91] Mothon, *Institutions Canoniques,* I, n. 252.

[92] Maroto, *Institutiones,* n. 572, II, A.

[93] Vromant, *De Negotiatione,* n. 21; also Vromant, *Ius Missionariorum,* II: *De Personis,* n. 414; Genicot-Salsmans, *Institutiones Theologiae Moralis,* II, n. 38.

[94] Wernz, *Ius Decretalium,* II, n. 219; Wernz-Vidal, *De Personis,* n. 128; Cappello, *Summa Iuris Canonici,* I, n. 247, 5; *cf.* also Canons 1521 to 1524.

[95] Salucci, *Diritto Penale,* II, n. 389, c.

if followed at all regularly, should be guarded cautiously and the opinion of the ordinary sought.[96]

Plenary Councils of Baltimore and Latin America

The Second and Third Plenary Councils of Baltimore enacted no new legislation on this subject and were content to repeat the legislation then in force in the universal Church, and now embodied in Canon 142.[97] The same legislation is to be found in the laws of the Plenary Council of Latin America held in 1899.[98]

Contract Not Invalidated by This Prohibition

Any form of trading contrary to the prohibition of Canon 142—excepting of course trading in Mass stipends—must be considered valid. This conclusion has been upheld consistently by the decisions of the Rota, and by the decretalists.[99]

Does the Exercise of Trading Require a Plurality of Acts?

Both Canon 142 and Canon 2380 are directed against the *exercise* of *trading*. Do these two words—*exercise* and *trading, negotiationem exercere*—imply, either individually or collectively, a plurality of actions, a certain practice or habit? Before presenting the opinion of canonists it is well to recall that neither of these words were introduced by the Code but are to be found in pre-Code legislation and in pre-Code canonical and theological authors.[100]

[96] For the attitude of the Holy See concerning the participation of clerics in such organizations as consumers' cooperatives the reader is referred to pages 31 and 34 and 35 in the chapter on the administration of lay property.

[97] *Concilii Plenarii Baltimorensis II Acta et Decreta*, n. 157; *Concilii Plenarii Baltimorensis III Acta et Decreta*, n. 82.

[98] *Acta et Decreta Concilii Plenarii Americae Latinae, in Urbe Celebrati Anno Domini MDCCCXCIX*, Romae, Typis Vaticanis, 1902, n. 652.

[99] *Sacrae Romanae Rotae Decisiones Recentiores*, decisio 378, nn. 5-9, partis 17; decisio 353, nn. 5 et 6, partis 19, tom. I; Pirhing, lib. III, tit. 50, 1, n. II; Benedict XIV, *De Synodo Dioecesana*, X, 6, 3; De Luca, *Theatrum Veritatis et Justitiae, de cambiis* disc. 18, n. 7.

[100] *Cf.* c. 15, X, *de vita et honestate clericorum*, III, 1. Practically all of the pre-Code authors quoted in the discussion of this point use similar expressions.

The opinions of authors may be grouped into three categories. The first group embraces those who say without any qualification that a practice—more than two or, as some say, three acts which must be morally united, that is, done with the intention of repetition—is required for an infringement of the law. These include Barbosa, Vermeersch-Creusen, Ojetti, Vromant, Augustine, Ciprotti, Chelodi, Lydon, and Cocchi.[101] These authors presume, of course, that the trading is in itself not dishonest.

A few authors hold that the law forbids even a single act. Bouuaert-Simenon express this opinion in the following terms: The obligation of abstaining from trading is *ex genere suo* grave; from grave sin light matter excuses which will be easily present, if there be only one or a few acts. On the other hand, although a trader properly speaking is one who *habitually* and *ex professo* engages in trading, nevertheless, even a single act is forbidden to clerics; this conclusion follows, they say, from the text and motives of the law. In treating of the penalties these two co-authors maintain that Canon 2380, because of the word *exercentes*, applies to *repeated* acts, although still insisting that a single act is forbidden to clerics.[102] De Meester quotes sources for similar opinions of a few pre-Code authors.[103]

A third group of authors require repeated acts, but not without some qualification. These authors consider the question from a moral, rather than from a strictly canonical, viewpoint. They consider the question of whether or not a cleric acting once or twice—some include a third time—can be said to be committing a mortal sin. The authors in this group say that the violation constitutes *a sin ex genere suo* grave, but that a cleric may be excused from mortal sin *ratione parvitatis materiae*, which may arise either from

[101] Barbosa, *Iuris Ecclesiastici Universi Libri Tres*, I, 40, n. 120; Vermeersch-Creusen, *Epitome*, I, n. 224, 2; Ojetti, *Commentarium*, III, 160; Vromant, *De Negotiatione*, n. 22, and also in *Ius Missionariorum*, II: *De Personis*, n. 415; Augustine, *Commentary*, II, 96; Pius Ciprotti, "De consummatione delictorum attento earum elemento obiectivo," p. 229—*Apollinaris*, VIII (1935), 224-248; Chelodi, *Jus Poenale*, n. 97, 5; Lydon, *Ready Answers in Canon Law*, p. 486; Cocchi, *Commentarium*, II, 140, 141.

[102] Bouuaert-Simenon, *Manuale*, I, n. 302, 3 and 4.

[103] De Meester, *Compendium*, I, n. 385, A.

the fewness of the acts of trading or from the inconsequential sums involved. When these two elements are found combined, all of these authors admit *parvitas materiae,* but they differ in their views if a considerable sum is involved, even in a single act.

Practically all of these authors admit that it is probable that no mortal sin is committed if a considerable sum be involved in a single act.[104] However, according to De Meester, a few pre-Code authors who, while they admitted *parvitas materiae* in a case where the act was done once or twice or three times, yet maintained that matter sufficient for the constitution of a mortal sin was present in a case when a single act involved a considerable value or sum of money.[105] Lehmkuhl distinguishes between a considerable sum and an enormous amount, claiming that the latter would constitute matter sufficiently grave for a mortal sin even in a single act.[106]

Others, particularly the decretalists, consider the *parvitas materiae* as arising from the fewness of the acts without any reference to the values involved. For example, Reiffenstuel, Schmalzgrueber, Pirhing and Ojetti, maintain that *parvitas materiae,* excusing from mortal sin, is had if the offense is committed only once or twice.[107]

Before presenting a summary of these various opinions it is well to note a few qualifications which some authors place on their opinions. For instance Schmalzgrueber says that a cleric who exercises the vocation of trading once or twice only ought to be excused *ratione parvitatis materiae* provided that *no scandal is given.*[108] It seems, therefore, that if scandal were given, he would not excuse

[104] St. Alphonsus, *Theologia Moralis,* III, n. 831; Ballerini-Palmieri, *Opus Theologicum Morale,* IV, 345; Genicot, *Theologiae Moralis Institutiones,* II, n. 38; Genicot-Salsmans, *Theologiae Moralis Institutiones,* II, n. 38; Aertnys-Damen, *Theologia Moralis,* I, n. 1137; A Coronata, *Institutiones,* I, n. 200; Cocchi, *Commentarium,* II, 140, 141; Cappello, *Summa Iuris Canonici,* I, n. 248; De Meester, *Compendium,* I, n. 385, A.

[105] De Meester, *Compendium* I, n. 385, A. De Meester is not accurate in quoting Ballerini-Palmieri and Genicot as following this opinion, neither does St. Alphonsus mention a case involving an enormous sum.

[106] Lehmkuhl, *Theologia Moralis,* I, n. 774, 4.

[107] Reiffenstuel, lib. III, tit. I, n. 134; Schmalzgrueber, lib. III, tit. 50, n. 16; Pirhing, lib. III, tit. 50, §1, n. III; Ojetti, *Commentarium,* III, 160.

[108] Schmalzgrueber, lib. III, tit. 50, n. 16.

the cleric even in a single offense. It was precisely scandal with its consequent detriment to the spread of the gospel that caused Clement IX to declare that a single offense on the part of missionaries made them subject to the full penalties of the law.[109]

St. Alphonsus likewise seems hesitant in excusing a cleric if scandal is given. He says that if a cleric trades only once or twice, in a matter not serious, *e. g.*, if he buys books, crosses, etc., in order to sell them for profit secretly, *occulte,* he does not sin mortally.[110] Ballerini-Palmieri repeat verbatim the words of St. Alphonsus and say that the word *occulte* refers precisely to the avoidance of scandal.[111] Cappello, likewise, states that a cleric sins only venially if he trades several times in light sums, or once in a considerable sum, provided that *contempt* and *scandal* are absent.[112]

A consideration of the opinions of these authors seems to lead to the inevitable conclusion that even a single act of trading is forbidden to clerics. Even those writers—and they are many—who hold that a mortal sin is not committed by a single act, in reality do admit that a single act is prohibited, since they admit that a single act is matter at least for a venial fault. The only basis for sin in this matter is the violation of a purely ecclesiastical law, since trading is not forbidden to clerics by the natural or positive divine law. Therefore, if an author admits that a venial sin is committed by a single act, then he necessarily admits that this is an infringement of the ecclesiastical law against trading. One might hesitate to say that a single act does constitute the exercise of trading, but the violation of some ecclesiastical law must be present in view of the opinion of so many authors that a single act does give rise to some offense. If this arises not from an offense against Canon 142, it must at least be considered as a violation of either Canon 138 or 139, § 1, prohibiting in general any act unbecoming or foreign to the clerical state. As quoted above, St. Alphonsus claims that trading is forbidden on the ground that it is unbecoming to the clerical state.

[109] *Cf.* above page 71.

[110] St. Alphonsus, *Theologia Moralis,* III, n. 831.

[111] Ballerini-Palmieri, *Opus Theologicum Morale,* IV, 345.

[112] Cappello, *Summa Iuris Canonici,* I, n. 248.

In agreement with many of these authors it seems certain that, if either scandal or contempt are present, then a single act would constitute a grave violation. This scandal is more likely to be present in regions where the Church is little known and where its very life depends on the unimpeachable example of its ministers. As stated before, this is the reason for the declaration of Clement IX, which expressly forbade even a single act of trading in mission territories and ordered the imposition of the usual severe penalties for such a single violation.

As stated above on page 71 this law was declared in force as late as 1883. A number of authors maintain that all territories are now governed by the law of the Code. Suffice it to say here that, though this is certainly true as regards penalties, it would seem that Clement's legislation is a declaration that grave scandal is caused against the Church by a single act of lucrative trading in mission lands. In consequence it would also seem that his interpretation—declared still in force as late as 1883 and recognized by all authors as effective up to the promulgation of the Code—should be considered as a norm today in mission lands. If even a small number of missionaries should engage in trading only once in a certain region, the result would be of grave detriment to the Church in the missions.

It is well to recall, too, that the authors who require habitual trading—more than two or three times—maintain that these acts must be morally, that is, by intention united. Could a missionary licitly trade at intervals, provided that he had no intention when planning each act to do so habitually? Suppose that a number of missionaries did likewise? To say that this is licit would be to defeat the purpose of the law. It would seem, therefore, that even a single act of trading in mission territories would be gravely illicit even today. However, the ordinary is granted the freedom of suiting the punishment to the gravity of the offense.

While speaking of penalties it might be opportune to remark here that the imposition of the severe pre-Code sanctions—though always *ferendae sententiae* except in missionary lands—was nevertheless obligatory on the ordinary and that this fact probably influenced some authors to condone a single offense. While admitting the presence of some fault, they nevertheless excused the cleric from all mandatory contraction of these severe penalties because of the fewness of the acts or the smallness of the sums involved. Now however, the ordinary would be justified, if contempt and scandal were absent, to issue a warning upon a first offense, particularly in territories other than mission districts.[113]

In the civil law of the United States an Indiana court maintained that *exercise* includes a single act. It decided that a statute forbidding the exercise of one's usual vocation on a Sunday was violated by a single act.[114]

WARNING NOT NECESSARY

St. Alphonsus rejects the opinion that a grave sin is not committed if, though without scandal, trading is carried on frequently but before a canonical admonition is given. With the Salmanticenses he teaches that the law clearly holds before the warning which was required only for the imposition of penalties. This warning, he continues, is not required as a condition necessary to establish the illicit character of the trading, for the latter is always forbidden as an act or practice which compromises the dignity and decorum of the clerical state.[115]

MINOR CLERICS INCLUDED IN THIS PROHIBITION

Vidal complains that Lehmkuhl and other modern authors liberate minor clerics from the prohibition against engaging in trading. As demonstrated on page 2, the Code understands as clerics all those who have received clerical tonsure. In the same place is explained the inclusion under this obligation of religious and those living a common life in a way similar to religious. In Wernz-Vidal the statement is also made that an oriental synod restricts this prohibition to clerics in major orders.[116]

[113] Penalties are discussed more in detail on pages 105-108.

[114] Voglesang v. State, 9 Ind. 112.

[115] St. Alphonsus, *Theologia Moralis*, III, n. 831.

[116] Wernz-Vidal, *De Personis*, n. 128, III, nota 33.

Causes Excusing From the Prohibition of Trading

All authorities admit that a cleric may practise trading if necessary for his own or his relatives' sustenance. Canon 142 is ecclesiastical law and, therefore, gives way to extreme necessity.

The common opinion that sufficient cause is had for an exemption not only if the necessities of life but also when the necessities of maintaining a decent status must be supplied, seems the more acceptable doctrine.[117] The reasons are first of all that a purely ecclesiastical law does not oblige under grave inconvenience, and secondly because a law enacted to prevent acts unbecoming to the clerical state should not be interpreted as necessitating other actions which would be unbecoming, such as begging, menial labor, etc.

In these cases, however, the necessity must be actual and, if possible, more becoming ways should be devised in which the cleric might provide, within the limits of true need, for his own sustenance and the sustenance of those to whom he is bound by natural ties.[118]

Clement XIII provided that if the cleric lived in Italy or on the adjacent islands permission must be secured from the Sacred Congregation of the Council; in remoter regions the same congregation could be petitioned, but the ordinary of the place was made fully competent.

Benedict XIV gave canonical sanction to a second form of necessity in his constitution *Apostolicae servitutis*. If an inherited business could not be disposed of immediately without temporal loss to the cleric he could, if he lived within Italy or on the adjacent islands, obtain from the Congregation of the Council permission to retain it for a time under the administration of a layman. If he lived in remoter regions, permission could be secured from the same congregation or from the ordinary of the place. If the cleric acted without such permission or ignored any of the above provisions, then he incurred all the penalties. Permission had to be obtained

[117] St. Alphonsus, *Theologia Moralis*, III, n. 837; Schmalzgrueber, lib. III, tit. 50, n. 16; Cocchi, *Commentarium*, II, 142, 143; Aertnys-Damen, *Theologia Moralis*, I, n. 1137; Cappello, *Summa Iuris Canonici*, I, n. 248, 3.

[118] Clemens XIII, ep. encycl. *"Cum primum,"* 17 sept., 1759, § 11—*Fontes*, n. 452; Schmalzgrueber, lib. III, tit. 50, n. 16.

even though the cleric inherited the business conjointly with other goods and other heirs and though it was administered in the name of another.[119]

Post-Code authors dispute as to whether the dispensation [120] for clerics living within Italy or on the adjacent islands must be sought from the Congregation of the Council or whether the local ordinary is competent. Benedict XIV required that the permission of the congregation be sought for these clerics if they should inherit a business which they cannot immediately dismiss without grave loss. Clement XIII made the same provision for clerics who had to supply the necessities of those to whom they were bound by natural ties. The basic dispute is whether the silence of the Code in the matter of dispensing removes the distinction between Italy and other regions, thereby making the ordinary competent throughout the world.

Vromant and Vermeersch-Creusen maintain that this silence of the Code makes the ordinary competent in all regions.[121] The following authors maintain that the provisions for securing permission as determined by Benedict XIV and Clement XIII are still in force: [122] Bastien, Maroto, Aertnys-Damen, Cocchi, Prümmer, A Coronata, Wernz-Vidal.[123]

[119] Benedictus XIV, const. "*Apostolicae servitutis,*" 25 febr., 1741, §§ 1, 2—*Fontes,* n. 306.

[120] A dispensation in the strict sense is not given, but rather a declaration as to the sufficiency of the excusing cause. *Cf.* Vermeersch-Creusen, *Epitome,* I, n. 224, 2.

[121] Vermeersch-Creusen, *Epitome,* I, n. 224, 2; Vromant, *Ius Missionariorum,* II: *De Personis,* n. 419; also Vromant, *De Negotiatione,* n. 29. Vromant (n. 28) would make the proper ordinary of religious competent for his subjects. These authors say that their opinion is in conformity with that of Monin expressed in *Action Catholique,* "Le Clergé et les operations financieres," 1920, pp. 449 ff.

[122] Some of these authors refer to the permission to carry on an inherited business, while others refer to permission in case of necessity. However, since the dispute has the same basis in both cases, namely, the silence of the Code, from analogy their opinions can be assumed to be identical for both cases.

[123] Bastien, *Directoire Canonique,* n. 518; Maroto, *Institutiones,* pp. 658, 659; Aertnys-Damen, *Theologia Moralis,* I, n. 1138; Cocchi, *Commentarium,* II, 141; Prümmer, *Manuale,* p. 98; A Coronata, *Institutiones,* I, n. 200; Wernz-Vidal, *De Personis,* n. 128, III.

A third opinion followed by a few authors deduces from the silence of the Code that the power of the ordinary has been taken away and that only the Holy See is competent to grant permission. This is the opinion of Blat, Cappello, De Meester, and Chelodi.[124]

The better opinion seems to be that of the majority, namely, that the silence of the Code does not affect any change in the matter of securing permission. As long, too, as a change in the law is doubtful the old law is to be considered in effect.[125] Therefore, in order to continue an inherited business, or to engage in trading in order to support those to whom the cleric is bound by natural ties, the Sacred Congregation of the Council should be consulted for those living in Italy and on the adjacent islands, while the local ordinary is competent in other regions. The same opinion would be applicable, it seems, if clerics should receive through donation some business concern. It is to be noted that both Benedict XIV and Clement XIII spoke of the ordinary of the place as being competent. No special provision was made for religious. It would seem that the proper ordinary of religious would be competent in regions outside of Italy and the adjacent islands.[126] However, if the religious superior should be the ordinary, it seems that it would be preferable to have recourse to the Sacred Congregation of Religious as soon as possible, since the benefits of the business would revert to the society. Such a course would prevent any suspicion of abuse.[127] In more urgent cases, of course, Canon 81 could be applied with the provisions which the Holy See is accustomed to demand as explained above.

[124] Blat, *Commentarium,* II, 108; Cappello, *Summa Iuris Canonici,* I, n. 248, 2; De Meester, *Compendium,* I, n. 388, n. 390; Chelodi, *Ius de Personis,* p. 212. Cappello and De Meester admit that in more urgent cases the ordinary is competent, but this is simply an application of Canon 81. Bouuaert-Simenon (*Manuale,* I, 181, nota 3)—inadvertently probably—say that the silence of the Code makes the ordinary competent everywhere as regards an inherited business, but deny this as regards necessity.

[125] Canon 6, 4°; Aertnys-Damen (*Theologia Moralis,* I, n. 1137), less accurately it would seem, refer to Canon 6, 2°.

[126] Vromant (*De Negotiatione,* n. 28) says that the proper ordinary of religious is competent.

[127] Bastien (*Directoire Canonique,* n. 518) says that it is necessary for religious to have recourse to the Congregation of Religious.

Some authors express the opinion that by custom a cleric may continue to carry on through others the business of his father, to which along with his brothers he has fallen heir.[128] Such a custom would seem to be licit provided that all the conditions required by the Code for the legitimacy of a custom be fulfilled, but only on the condition and as long as the business is the joint possession of the brothers and is exercised as such.[129] It is well to note here that popes have condemned in the strongest language any custom contrary to the provisions of the canons.[130] Such condemnation may be taken as a warning but, of course, has not the force of the reprobation of Canon 5.

A number of cases are on record in which the Holy See has granted a dispensation or rather a favorable declaration allowing clerics to carry on businesses through others. A number of these can be found in the decisions of the Congregation of the Council and of the Congregation of Bishops and Regulars.[131]

Any favorable declaration in this matter must be considered null and revoked and the business must be given up as soon as the needs of the cleric or of his relatives cease, or other legitimate means present themselves of providing for them.[132]

Stocks and Bonds

After the middle of the past century doubts began to arise as to the licitness of clerics purchasing stocks *(actiones)* and bonds

[128] Cocchi, *Commentarium,* II, 141; D'Annibale, *Summula,* III, n. 156, nota 12; Genicot, *Theologiae Moralis Institutiones,* II, 38; Maroto, *Institutiones,* p. 659, nota 1, who quotes Bucceroni as of the same opinion.

[129] Cappello, *Summa Iuris Canonici,* I, n. 248, 2, nota 17.

[130] *Cf.* especially Clemens XIII, ep. encycl. *"Cum primum,"* 17, sept., 1759—*Fontes,* n. 452, § 4.

[131] Pallottini, Salvator, *Collectio Omnium Conclusionum et Resolutionum, S. C. C.,* 17 vols., Romae, 1868-1893, "Presbiteri Simplices," III: "presbiteri simplices et clerici seu ecclesiastici in genere quoad negotiationem et venationem," nn. 11-16; *cf.* etiam "Est-il Permis aux Ecclesiastiques d'Acheter des Actions de Societes Industrielles," *Nouvelle Revue Théologique,* VI (1874), 518-539; Lingen-Reuss, *Causae Selectae,* pp. 151-155.

[132] Clemens XIII, ep. encycl. *"Cum primum,"* 17 sept., 1759—*Fontes,* n. 452, § 11; De Meester, *Compendium,* I, n. 390; Blat, *Commentarium,* II, 108.

(obligationes). In regard to the latter there was little difficulty since bonds are practically equivalent to a loan with a determined rate of interest. The bondholder has no share, neither directly nor indirectly, in the ownership or administration of the company. All authors allow the purchasing of bonds.

As regards stocks, however, a prolonged discussion ensued in view of the fact that a stockholder becomes a part owner of the company and as such is entitled to a proportionate vote in its affairs. The opinion of authors may be summed up under three headings: First are those who teach that clerics may not buy stocks in any commercial or industrial companies. The former companies engage clearly in trading forbidden to clerics, while the latter companies—granted that the articles purchased are changed through hired labor—are also engaged in forbidden actions. Nor does it matter that the actions are done through others, for this is likewise forbidden by the canon. This is the opinion expressed by Lehmkuhl, D'Annibale and others.[183]

The second opinion adopts a distinction between companies which engage in occupations forbidden to clerics and those that perform actions not forbidden. According to this opinion clerics may not purchase stocks in strictly commercial companies, but can do so in companies which engage in those forms of artificial or industrial trading which are not forbidden to clerics, such a mines, railroads, cattle-raising, etc., as explained in preceding pages. This is the opinion of Wernz, Vidal, and Craisson.[184]

The third and today by far the more common opinion maintains

[183] Lehmkuhl, *Institutiones,* II, n. 612; D'Annibale, *Summula,* III, n. 157; De Meester (*Compendium,* I, 274, nota 3) quotes others of the same opinion.

[184] Wernz, *Ius Decretalium,* II, n. 219, ad scholion; Wernz-Vidal, *De Personis,* n. 128, ad scholion—Vidal says that the opinion is doubtful, *dubio iuris,* and therefore the third opinion may be followed; Craisson, "Est-il permis aux Ecclésiastiques et aux Communautés religieuses d'acquérir ou de garder des actions dans les societés commerciales ou industrielles?" *Revue des Sciences Ecclésiastiques,* XIII (1866), 460-483. Craisson would forbid also the purchasing of stocks in banks since they engage at times in trading forbidden to clerics. Chelodi (*Jus Poenale,* n. 97, 5) says the holding of stocks in commercial companies is illicit, but in *Ius de Personis* (pp. 212, 213) allows the buying of stocks in all companies.

that clerics may purchase stocks in all forms of companies. The following embrace this view: A Coronata, Augustine, Bargilliat, Bouuaert-Simenon, Cappello, Cocchi, De Meester, Kinane, Maroto, Raus, Vermeersch-Creusen.[135] This opinion is substantiated first of all by positive declarations of the Holy See which have evolved from a general prohibition to an indult granted in a particular case and finally to a general permission under certain precautions obviating abuses and dangers.[136]

(a) In 1846 the Congregation of Bishops and Regulars received the following questions:

"I. Utrum clericis in SS. ordinibus constitutis vel beneficium habentibus actiones acquirere liceat commendatariae societatis Civitatis Castelli in casu?—Et quatenus negative; II. Utrum supplicendum sit Sanctitati Suae pro benigno indulto?" The congregation responded: "Ad I: Non licere. Ad II: Provisum in primo." [137]

(b) In 1857 the Holy Office gave a response by which the pope granted the faculties to bishops, to be communicated through the Congregation of Bishops, to permit ecclesiastics to purchase stocks in railroads with their own money.[138] In 1841 an indult of Gregory XVI allowed a priest, with the acquiescence of his ordinary, to retain for five years a certain number of stocks in a manufacturing company.[139] These declarations indicate the desire of the Holy See

[135] A Coronata, *Institutiones,* I, n. 200; Augustine, *Commentary,* II, 97; Bargilliat, *Praelectiones,* I, n. 439, e; Bouuaert-Simenon, *Manuale,* I, n. 303, B; Cappello, *Summa Iuris Canonici,* I, n. 248, 4; Cocchi, *Commentarium,* II, 142; De Meester, *Compendium,* I, 275—De Meester quotes other authors of the same opinion; Kinane, J., "May Priests Invest Money in Industrial and Commercial Companies?," *Irish Ecclesiastical Record,* XXI (1928), 417-421; Maroto, *Institutiones,* n. 572, III; Raus, *Institutiones Canonicae,* p. 118; Vermeersch-Creusen, *Epitome,* I, n. 224, 3.

[136] De Meester (*Compendium,* I, 275, nota 3) finds a parallel development in the Holy See's attitude towards the contract of loan.

[137] S. C. Ep. and Reg., *Causa civitatis Castelli,* 30 ian., 1846; Bizzari, *Collectanea,* p. 530.

[138] S. C. S. Off., 1 apr., 1857—*Nouvelle Revue Théologique,* XXV (1893), 607.

[139] *Analecta Juris Pontif.,* Ser. VII, col. 494s—quoted by De Meester, *Compendium,* I, 275, nota 5.

at that time to make temporary provisions rather than to settle the controversy immediately.

(c) Of greater force is the response of the Holy Office given November 17, 1875:

"Non esse inquietandos qui nomina seu actiones viarum ferrearum similiumque societatum aut arcarum publicae utilitati inservientium de sua pecunia acquirunt, dummodo parati sint stare mandatis Sedis Apostolicae, et certo sciant eas societates nullum habere propositum finem illicitum vel quomodolibet suspectum, et dummodo nullam in eis societatibus administrationis partem suscipiant, neque actionum earumdem societatum negotiationem exerceant."[140] A later response of the Holy Office is of still greater value for it allows the buying of stocks in banks which in turn engage in all forms of trading: "Juxta exposita et attentis peculiaribus temporum circumstantiis, personas ecclesiasticas non esse inquietandos si emerint aut emant actiones seu titulos mensae nummulariae, dummodo paratae sint stare mandatis S. Sedis, et se abstineant a qualibet negotiatione dictarum actionum seu titulorum, et praesertim ab omni contractu qui speciem habeat ut vulgo dicitur 'dei giuochi di borsa'."[141] Since these responses make no distinction between strictly commercial and other companies and as they are of a general nature it is a safe conclusion that a cleric may buy stocks in all societies as long as he observes the safeguards enumerated. At least a *dubium iuris* is present which makes the opinion certain in practice if not in theory.

A second argument is derived from the fact that in other places where the Code speaks of stocks and bonds under the general terms of *tituli,* no distinction is made concerning stocks in strictly commercial and industrial companies.[142]

Authors deduce a third argument from the original draft of Canon 142, which contained a second paragraph, quoted by Maroto as follows:

> Licet tamen clericis obligationes vel actiones societatum industrialium vel commercialium aut arcarum publicae

[140] *Cf. Nouvelle Revue Théologique,* XXV (1893), 609.

[141] This response was quoted by the Congregation for the Propagation of the Faith: litt. (ad Ep. Ruraemunden.), 7 iul., 1893—*Fontes,* n. 4925.

[142] *Cf.* Canons 594, 1539, § 2.

utilitati inservientium emere, dummodo eae societates nullum habeant propositum finem illicitum vel quomodolibet suspectum neque clerici iisdem actionibus aut obligationibus negotiationem exerceant.[143]

These authors maintain that this second paragraph was omitted because it was already contained implicitly in the original first paragraph which is identical with Canon 142 as it stands in the Code, and because the Holy See was not desirous of approving universally a practice which depends a great deal on circumstances of time and place. By not expressly granting general freedom in this matter the Code leaves the way open for particular legislation to control possible abuses.

The final argument is taken from the purpose of the law of Canon 142 which, as demonstrated above, is to prevent scandal and the over-solicitude of clerics with secular affairs to the detriment of their duties. As stock companies are now constituted the stockholders have no immediate part in the business and are not commonly considered to be engaged in business, nor does the proper or wrong administration reflect merit or condemnation on the stockholders. Such remote participation does not make the stockholder *per se* so solicitous of the varying fortunes of the business.[144]

In the responses mentioned above no limitation is placed on the number of stocks that might be purchased, but it would hardly be the intention of the Holy See to allow the purchasing or retention of such a large number of stocks or bonds as would almost necessarily involve clerics in all the risks, gains and anxieties of the business.[145]

There might be some dispute as to the licitness of a cleric becoming one of the founders of a company to be established. The responses of the Holy See make no distinction between companies already constituted and those to be constituted, but it would seem

[143] Maroto, *Institutiones* (I, 657), Ayrinhac (*General Legislation*, p. 313), and A Coronata (*Institutiones*, I, n. 200) give, in substance, the same quotation.

[144] Vermeersch-Creusen, *Epitome*, I, n. 224, 3; Maroto, *Institutiones*, I, 656; De Meester, *Compendium*, I, 277, 278.

[145] Bouuaert-Simenon, *Manuale*, I, n. 303, B; De Meester, *Compendium*, I, 272, nota 1.

more advisable, although not strictly forbidden, for clerics to abstain from taking a prominent part in the organization of a company.[146] The purchasing of stocks, however, in such a company seems licit.

As is evident, a cleric may not accept any part in the administration of such companies. This is clear from the responses above and is the unanimous opinion of authors.[147] It seems licit for a cleric to be present at a meeting of the stockholders—provided no scandal is given—called for the purpose of electing proper officials, but not for the actual government of the business. However, it is preferable that clerics be represented at such meetings by proxies, as is the custom.[148]

In view of the above responses it seems hardly necessary to insist on the absolute prohibition of any form of forbidden lucrative trading in stocks or bonds. The Holy Office insisted that clerics abstain *praesertim ab omni contractu qui speciem habeat ut vulgo dicitur "dei giuochi di borsa."* [149] Canon 1539, § 2, permits administrators to exchange *titulos ad latorem . . . in alios titulos . . . exclusa qualibet commercii vel negotiationis specie* . . . It is well to note that in both these instances the Holy See employed the term *species* which is the same term employed in Canon 827 in treating of the important prohibition against simoniacal trading in Mass stipends: *A stipe Missarum quaelibet etiam species negotiationis vel mercaturae omnino arceatur.* The fact that such trading is carried on through an agent does not lessen the guilt of the cleric.

Clerics, of course, are not forbidden the prudent administration of their possessions in this matter. Excluding, therefore, any form of purchasing and selling merely for the purpose of gain, a cleric for some honest reason, may sell his stocks or bonds, not only once or twice, but even frequently, provided that this does not exceed the limits of domestic trading as outlined above on pages 78 and 79.[150]

[146] Cappello, *Summa Iuris Canonici,* I, n. 248, 4.

[147] *Cf.* also Chapter V on the administration of lay property.

[148] Vermeersch-Creusen, *Epitome,* I, n. 224, 3; A Coronata, *Institutiones,* I, n. 200.

[149] *Fontes,* n. 4925.

[150] Aertnys-Damen, *Theologia Moralis,* I, n. 1139; Maroto, *Institutiones,* n. 572, III.

A cleric could not, therefore, turn over a sum of money to an agent with instruction to use it for the purpose of trading in stocks and bonds in order to reap profit from such transactions. The form of trading on the exchange, as outlined above on page 67, in which the purchaser does not intend to accept actual possession of the stocks or bonds, but merely to reap the profit, or suffer the possible loss, arising in view of the difference in the exchange quotation on the day of agreement from that of the future day determined for the actual delivery of the instruments, is clearly illicit.

Solemnities of Alienation

In the alienation of stocks and bonds which pertain to a moral ecclesiastical person all the solemnities of Canons 1530 to 1532 must be observed.[151] Considering the provisions of Canon 1539 the exchange of such instruments for others equally safe and productive is not to be compared to true alienation. The prescriptions of Canon 1539, however, must be strictly observed.[152]

Particular Legislation

According to Vromant particular councils have frequently urged the prohibition against engaging in any form of *playing the exchange*. He refers, however, only to the Fourth Provincial Council of Malines.[153] The Baltimore Councils make no mention of such transactions.

Penalties

The penalties which have been enacted throughout the centuries against clerics engaging in forbidden forms of trading are found in the historical introduction to this chapter, but it might be helpful to summarize them here. From the very beginning the severest sanctions have been urged against those delinquent in this matter. Such punishments as excommunication, suspension and degradation—

[151] S. C. C., 17 febr., 1906, *Collectanea* (ed. 1907), n. 2229; A Coronata, *Institutiones*, I, n. 200.

[152] Vromant, *De Negotiatione*, n. 32; A Coronata, *Institutiones*, I, n. 200.

[153] Vromant, *De Negotiatione*, n. 7.

as they were understood in the early days of the Church—were enacted from the time of the Apostolic Canons, were repeated by the Council of Trent, and were in vogue up to the time of the Code. These penalties were especially urged in missionary lands, and superiors were required to punish delinquents under the threat of incurring themselves the same severe penalties. The severity of these penalties demonstrates that the prohibition was considered to bind under pain of mortal sin. The gain acquired through such trading was subject to confiscation by Church authorities.

All these penalties throughout the history of the Church have been *ferendae sententiae,* except those applying to the missionary lands outlined above which were expressly declared to be *latae sententiae.*[154] Obviously the penalty of Canon 2380 is also to be imposed *ferendae sententiae* since the ordinary has to select the proper punishment.[155] Even the punishments against those trading in Mass stipends are *ferendae sententiae.*[156]

The ordinary of Canon 2380 is, of course, the proper ordinary. The ordinary of the place, therefore, is competent for all except exempt religious, who are subject to their own superior having the powers of an ordinary.[157]

Does the Code Abrogate Former Punishments Against Missionaries?

The universal opinion of authors is that the silence of the Code in regard to the former sanctions against missionaries engaging in trading automatically terminates these severe punishments.[158] This interpretation is justified by virtue of the principle enunciated

[154] Salucci, *Diritto Penale,* II, n. 388; Pistocchi, *I Canoni Penali,* p. 291.

[155] Vromant, *De Negotiatione,* n. 18; A Coronata, *Institutiones,* I, n. 200.

[156] Canon 2324.

[157] Vromant, *De Negotiatione,* n. 18; Fanfani, *De Iure Religiosorum,* p. 356.

[158] Cocchi, *Commentarium,* II, 143; Vromant, *De Negotiatione,* n. 12; Vromant, *Ius Missionariorum,* II: *De Personis,* n. 409; Wernz-Vidal, *De Personis,* n. 128, IV; De Meester, *Compendium,* I, n. 385, nota 5; Bouuaert-Simenon, *Manuale,* I, n. 302, 3, nota 5; Pistocchi, *I Canoni Penali,* p. 293; Chelodi, *Ius Poenale,* n. 97, 5; Prümmer, *Manuale,* p. 98; Vermeersch-Creusen, *Epitome,* III, n. 584; Blat, *Commentarium,* II, 106; Augustine, *Commentary,* VIII, 461.

in Canon 6, 5°. For the same reason the former spoliation of goods gained through forbidden trading in favor of the *Camera Apostolica* must also be considered abrogated.[159]

In view of the doubt explained in detail above on pages 90 to 95, as to whether or not the expression *negotiationem exercere* requires a habit of at least two or three offenses morally united, Canon 2380 should not be applied until the doubt has been solved. However, the ordinary, if he judges it prudent, can apply Canon 2222.

Under past legislation the fact that the trading was carried on through others or for the benefit of others did not lessen the penalties to be imposed.[160] The same interpretations hold today. Indeed Pistocchi regards the intervention of another as aggravating the offense.[161]

It would seem that the ordinary is under the obligation of punishing clerics who violate the prohibition against trading. Canon 2380 employs the term *coerceantur*. This is the opinion expressed clearly by Cappello, Mothon, Salucci and Augustine.[162] Chelodi and Bastien, while saying that the ordinary has the power to inflict the punishments, do not state that he is obliged to do so.[163] However, the ordinary could abstain from inflicting the punishment according to his prudent judgment, or if the offender is truly contrite and has repaired the scandal given.[164] Canon 2380 does not require necessarily a canonical warning before the imposition of a penalty.

The punishment selected by the ordinary should be in proportion to the gravity of the offense. He should consider all the circumstances regarding the offending cleric, the sums involved, the number

[159] Benedict XIV, *cf.* const. "*Apostolicae servitutis,*" 25 febr. 1741—*Fontes,* n. 306; *cf.* also Schmalzgrueber, lib. III, tit. 50, n. 33.

[160] Wernz, *Ius Decretalium,* II, n. 219, III.

[161] Pistocchi, *I Canoni Penali,* p. 291.

[162] Cappello, *Summa Iuris Canonici,* I, n. 248, 6; Mothon, *Institutions Canoniques,* I, n. 251; Salucci, *Diritto Penale,* II, n. 389; Augustine, *Commentary,* VIII, p. 462.

[163] Chelodi, *Ius de Personis,* p. 213; Bastien, *Directoire Canonique,* n. 518.

[164] Bouuaert-Simenon, *Manuale,* I, n. 302, 4; Canon 2223, § 3; also § 3, 2°.

of offenses, the scandal given, etc. He should be careful to ascertain: (1) That the transaction falls under one of the forbidden forms of trading. (2) That permission was not secured or that one of the excusing causes was not present. (3) That the transaction is not merely domestic trading. (4) That the offense is not doubtful according to approved authors.[165]

The graver penalties of suspension, and especially excommunication, should not be imposed unless grave scandal is to be repaired or persistent contumaciousness is to be broken. In most cases privation, at least for a time, of ecclesiastical offices or of jurisdiction for hearing confessions would seem sufficient.[166] Because of his vows a religious offending in this matter should be punished more severely than a secular cleric.

Since trading has always been considered an occupation foreign to the clerical state, Canon 2379 is also applicable in this matter. Therefore, if a cleric should fail to wear the ecclesiastical garb and refuse to comply with the warnings authoritatively and repeatedly administered, as prescribed by this canon, he is eventually to be deposed.[167]

By virtue of Canon 987, 3°, a cleric would become subject to a simple impediment to Holy Orders, if he should accept an office or take an administrative part in forbidden trading, until he has given up his office or administration and rendered an account and so become free from such entanglements.[168]

[165] Pistocchi, *I Canoni Penali*, p. 292.

[166] Vermeersch-Creusen, *Epitome*, III, n. 584; Pistocchi, *I Canoni Penali*, p. 293; Augustine, *Commentary*, VIII, 462.

[167] Pistocchi, *I Canoni Penali*, p. 288; *cf.* above pages 17, 18 for a fuller treatment of this canon.

[168] *Cf.* above pages 4-7 for a fuller treatment of this impediment.

BIBLIOGRAPHY

Sources

Acta Apostolicae Sedis, Romae, 1909-

Acta Sanctae Sedis, 41 vols., Romae, 1865-1908.

Codex Iuris Canonici Pii X Pontificis Maximi iussu digestus, Benedicti Papae XV auctoritate promulgatus, Romae, 1918.

Codex Theodosianus, ed. P. Krueger-Th. Mommsen, 3 vols., Berolini, 1905.

Codicis Iuris Canonici Fontes, cura Emi. Petri Card. Gasparri editi, 7 vols., Romae, 1923-

Collectanea in usum Secretariae Sacrae Congregationis Episcoporum et Regularium, ed. Bizzari, Romae, 1885.

Collectanea S. Congregationis de Propaganda Fide, Romae, 1893.

Collectanea S. Congregationis de Propaganda Fide, 2 vols., Romae, 1907.

Concilii Plenarii Americae Latinae in Urbe Celebrati Anno Domini 1899, Acta et Decreta, 2 vols., Romae, 1902.

Concilii Plenarii Baltimorensis II (1866) Acta et Decreta, Baltimorae: typis Joannes Murphy et Sociorum, 1868.

Concilii Plenarii Baltimorensis III (1884) Acta et Decreta, Baltimorae: typis Joannes Murphy et Sociorum, 1886.

Concilii Tridentini, Canones et Decreta, ed. Richter-Schulte, Lipsiae, 1853.

Corpus Iuris Canonici, editio Lipsiensis secunda post Aemilii Freidberg, 2 vols., Lipsiae, 1879-1881.

Corpus Iuris Civilis, 3 vols., Berolini, 1928-1929.

Institutiones, quas recognovit P. Krueger.

Digesta, quae recognovit T. Mommsen et retractavit P. Krueger.

Codex Iustinianus, quem recongovit et retractavit P. Krueger.

Novellae, quas recognovit R. Schoell et absolvit G. Kroll.

Decretum Gratiani emendatum et notionibus illustratum, una cum glossis, Gregorii XIII Pont. Max. iussu editum, 2 vols., Romae, 1852.

Lingen, C.-Reuss, P., *Causae Selectae in S. Congregatione Cardinalium Concilii Tridentini Interpretum ab 1823-1869*, Parisiis, 1871.

Mansi, Joannes Dominicus, *Sacrorum Conciliorum Nova et Amplissima Collectio*, 51 vols., Florentiae, 1859.

Pallottini, Salvator, *Collectio Omnium Conclusionum et Resolutionum apud Sacram Congregationem Cardinalium Sacri Concilii Tridentini*, 17 vols., Romae, 1868-1893.

Sacrae Romanae Rotae Decisiones Recentiores, Paulus Rubeus, Romae.

Authors

A Coronata, Mattheus Conte, *Institutiones Iuris Canonici ad Usum Utriusque Cleri et Scholarum*, 4 vols., Taurini: Marietti, 1928.

Aertnys, J.-Damen, C., *Theologia Moralis*, 11. ed., 2 vols., Taurinorum Augustae: Marietti, 1928.

Aichner, Simon, *Compendium Iuris Ecclesiastici,* 6. ed., Brixinae, 1887.

Ayrinhac, H. A., *General Legislation in the New Code of Canan Law,* New York: Blase Benziger & Co., 1923.

———, *Legislation on the Sacraments in the New Code of Canon Law,* New York: Blase Benziger & Co., 1923.

———, *Penal Legislation in the New Code of Canon Law,* New York: Blase Benziger & Co., 1920.

[Bachofen] Augustine, Charles, *A Commentary on the New Code of Canon Law,* 3. ed., 8 vols., St. Louis: B. Herder Book Co., 1918-1922.

Ballerini, Antonius-Palmieri, Dominicus, *Opus Theologicum Morale,* 3. ed., 7 vols., Prati, 1898-1901.

Barbosa, Augustinus, *Iuris Ecclesiastici Universi Libri Tres,* Lugduni, 1660.

Bargilliat, M., *Praelectiones Juris Canonici,* 37. ed., Parisiis: Apud Baston Berche et Pagis, 1923-1924.

Bastien, Pierre, *Directoire Canonique a l'Usage des Congregations a Voeux Simples,* 3. ed., Bruges: Ch. Beyaert, 1923.

Benedictus XIV, *De Synodo Dioecesana,* 2 vols., Romae, 1806.

Blat, Albertus, *Commentarium Textus Codicis Iuris Canonici,* 6 vols., Romae: ex typographia Pontificia in Instituto Pii X, 1921-1927.

Bouix, D., *Tractatus de Principiis Iuris Canonici,* Parisiis, 1882.

Bouuaert, F. C.-Simenon, G., *Manuale Juris Canonici ad Usum Seminariorum,* 3 vols., Wetteren: De Meester et fils, 1930.

Cappello, Felix M., *Summa Iuris Canonici,* 2. ed., 2 vols., Romae: Apud Aedes Universitatis Gregorianae, 1932.

———, *Summa Iuris Publici Ecclesiastici,* 3. ed., Romae: Apud Aedes Universitatis Gregorianae, 1932.

———, *Tractatus Canonico-Moralis De Sacramentis,* Vol. II, pars III: *De Sacra Ordinatione,* Taurinorum Augustae: Marietti, 1935.

Catholic Encyclopedia, The, edited by Charles G. Herberman, Edward A. Pace, Condé B. Pallen, Thomas J. Shahan, John J. Wynne, assisted by numerous collaborators, 15 vols., New York: Robert Appleton Co., 1907.

Chelodi, Ioannes, *Ius De Personis Iuxta Codicem Iuris Canonici,* 2. ed., Tridenti: Libr. Edit. Tridentum, 1927.

———, *Ius Poenale et Ordo Procedendi in Iudiciis Criminalibus Iuxta Codicem Iuris Canonici,* Tridenti: Libr. Edit. Tridentum, 1925.

Cicognani, Amleto G., *Canon Law,* translated by Joseph M. O'Hara and Francis Brennan, Philadelphia: The Dolphin Press, 1934.

Cocchi, Guidus, *Commentarium in Codicem Iuris Canonici ad Usum Scholarum,* 2. and 3. ed., 8 vols., Taurinorum Augustae: Marietti, 1925-1932.

D'Annibale, Josephus, *Summula Theologiae Moralis,* 3. ed., 3 vols., Romae, 1892.

De Luca, Ioannes, *Theatrum Veritatis et Justitiae, sive Decisivi Discursus,* 16 vols., Coloniae Agrippinae, 1706.

De Lugo, Ioannes, *De Iustitia et Iure,* 2 vols., Lugduni, 1670.

De Meester, A., *Juris Canonici et Juris Canonico-Civilis Compendium,* 2. ed., 3 vols., Bruges: Ex typis Societatis Sancti Augustini, 1921-1928.

Fagnanus, Prosper, *Commentaria in Quinque Libros Decretalium*, 4 vols., Venetiis, 1696.

Fanfani, Ludovicus, *De Iure Religiosorum ad Normam Codicis Iuris Canonici*, 2. ed., Taurini and Romae: Marietti, 1925.

Ferraris, F. Lucius, *Bibliotheca Canonica Iuridica Moralis Theologica nec non Ascetica Polemica Rubricistica Historica*, ed. novissima, 9 vols., Romae, 1891.

Gasparri, Petrus, *Tractatus Canonicus De Sacra Ordinatione*, 2 vols., Parisiis and Lugduni, 1893-1894.

Genicot, Eduardus, *Theologiae Moralis Institutiones*, 2 vols., Lovanii, 1897.

Genicot, Eduardus-Salsmans, I., *Theologiae Moralis Institutiones*, 10. ed., 2 vols., Bruxellis: Dewit, 1922.

Hefele, C. J., *A History of the Christian Councils*, translated by William R. Clark, 2. ed., 5 vols., Edinburgh, 1883-1896.

Hickey, John J., *Irregularities and Simple Impediments in the New Code of Canon Law*, The Catholic University of America, Canon Law Studies, n. 7, Washington: The Catholic University of America, 1920.

Hostiensis [Henricus de Segusio], *Commentaria in Quartum Librum Decretalium*, Venetiis, 1581.

Keller, Charles F., *Mass Stipends*, The Catholic University of America, Canon Law Studies, n. 27, Washington: The Catholic University of America, 1925.

Lehmkuhl, Augustinus, *Theologia Moralis*, 12. ed., Freiburg in Breisgau: B. Herder & Co., 2 vols., 1914.

Liguori, S. Alphonsus, *Theologia Moralis*, ed. nova—Gaudé, 4 tomes, Romae: Ex typographia Vaticana, 1905-1912.

Lydon, P. J., *Ready Answers in Canon Law*, New York: Benziger Brothers, 1934.

Maroto, Philippus, *Institutiones Iuris Canonici*, 3. ed., 2 vols., Romae: Commentarium pro Religiosis, 1921.

Monacelli, F., *Formularium Legale Praticum Fori Ecclesiastici*, 4 vols., Venetiis, 1706.

Mothon, Joseph Pie, *Institutions Canoniques*, 2 vols., Paris: Société Saint-Augustin, Desclée, De Brouwer & Cie, 1922-1924.

Ojetti, B., *Commentarium in Codicem Iuris Canonici*, 4 vols., Romae: Apud Aedes Universitatis Gregorianae, 1927-1931.

Pignatelli, Jacobus, *Consultationes Canonicae*, 11 vols., Coloniae Allobrogum, 1700.

Pirhing, Henricus, *Ius Canonicum in V Libros Decretalium*, 5 vols., Dilingae, 1674-1678.

Pistocchi, Mario, *I Canoni Penali del Codice Ecclesiastico*, Torino e Roma: Marietti, 1925.

Prümmer, Dominicus, *Manuale Theologiae Moralis Secundum Principia S. Thomae Aquinatis in Usum Scholarum*, 6. ed., 3 vols., Friburgi Brisgoviae: B. Herder & Co., 1928.

Raus, P. J. B., *Institutiones Canonicae,* Lugduni and Parisiis: Typis Emmanuelis Vitte, 1923.

Reiffenstuel, Anacletus, *Ius Canonicum Universum,* 4 vols., Romae, 1843-1844.

Salucci, Raffaele, *Il Diritto Penale Secondo Il Codice di Diritto Canonico,* 2 vols., Subiaco: Tipografia dei Monasteri, 1926.

Schäfer, Timotheus, *Compendium De Religiosis ad Normam Codicis Iuris Canonici,* 2. ed., Münster i. W: Ex Officina Libraria Aschendorff, 1931.

Schmalzgrueber, Franciscus, *Ius Ecclesiasticum Universum,* 4 vols., Romae, 1843-1844.

Smith, S. B., *Elements of Ecclesiastical Law,* 2 vols., New York, 1882.

Vermeersch, A.-Creusen, J., *Epitomé Iuris Canonici cum Commentariis ad Scholas et ad Usum Privatum,* 2. and 3. ed., 3 vols., Romae: H. Dessain, 1925-1927.

Vromant, G., *De Negotiatione Clericis et Religiosis Interdicta,* Monographiae Juridicae Ex Ephemeride *Jus Pontificium* Excerptae Eiusve Cura Editae, series II, fasc. IV, Romae: Jus Pontificium, 1929.

———, *Ius Missionariorum,* 5 tomes, Louvain: Museum Lessianum, 1929-1931.

Wernz, Franciscus, *Ius Decretalium,* 6 vols., Romae, 1908-1913.

Wernz, Franciscus-Vidal, Petrus, *Ius Canonicum ad Codicis Normam Exactum,* 1. and 3. ed., 6 tomes, Romae: Apud Aedes Universitatis Gregorianae, 1928-1935.

Zollmann, Carl, *American Church Law,* St. Paul: West Publishing Co., 1933.

Periodicals

American Ecclesiastical Review, The, Philadelphia, 1889-

Apollinaris Commentarium Iuridico-Canonicum, Romae, 1928-

Archiv für katholisches Kirchenrecht, Mainz, 1857-

Commentarium pro Religiosis, Romae, 1920-

Irish Ecclesiastical Record, Dublin, 1864-

Jus Pontificium, Romae, 1921-

Monitore Ecclesiastico, Il, Rome, 1888-

Nouvelle Revue Théologique, Paris, 1868-

Periodica de Re Canonica et Morali, Romae et Brugis, 1905-

Revue des Sciences Ecclesiastiques, Paris, 1860-

ALPHABETICAL INDEX

BIOGRAPHICAL NOTE

Joseph Bernard Brunini was born July 24, 1909, at Vicksburg, Mississippi, where he received his elementary schooling at St. Francis Xavier Academy and St. Aloysius High School. From Georgetown University, Washington, D. C., he received the degree of Bachelor of Arts in 1930. In the fall of the same year he entered the North American College in Rome for his theological training. From the Propaganda University in Rome he received the degree of Bachelor of Sacred Theology. He was ordained to the priesthood on December 5, 1933. In September, 1934, he enrolled in the School of Canon Law at the Catholic University of America, from which institution he received the degree of Bachelor of Canon Law in 1935, and the Licentiate in 1936.

CANON LAW STUDIES

1. Freriks, Rev. Celestine A., C.PP.S., J.C.D., Religious Congregations in Their External Relations, 121 pp., 1916.
2. Galliher, Rev. Daniel M., O.P., J.C.D., Canonical Elections, 117 pp., 1917.
3. Borkowski, Rev. Aurelius L., O.F.M., J.C.D., De Confraternitatibus Ecclesiasticis, 136 pp., 1918.
4. Castillo, Rev. Cayo, J.C.D., Disertacion Historico-Canonica sobre la Potestad del Cabildo en Sede Vacante o Impedida del Vicario Capitular, 99 pp., 1919 (1918).
5. Kubelbeck, Rev. William J., S.T.B., J.C.D., The Sacred Penitentiaria and Its Relation to Faculties of Ordinaries and Priests, 129 pp., 1918.
6. Petrovits, Rev. Joseph, J.C., S.T.D., J.C.D., The New Church Law on Matrimony, X-461 pp., 1919.
7. Hickey, Rev. John J., S.T.B., J.C.D., Irregularities and Simple Impediments in the New Code of Canon Law, 100 pp., 1920.
8. Klekotka, Rev. Peter J., S.T.B., J.C.D., Diocesan Consultors, 179 pp., 1920.
9. Wanenmacher, Rev. Francis, J.C.D., The Evidence in Ecclesiastical Procedure Affecting the Marriage Bond, 1920 (Printed 1935).
10. Golden, Rev. Henry Francis, J.C.D., Parochial Benefices in the New Code, IV-119 pp., 1921 (Printed 1925).
11. Koudelka, Rev. Charles J., J.C.D., Pastors, Their Rights and Duties According to the New Code of Canon Law, 211 pp., 1921.
12. Melo, Rev. Antonius, O.F.M., J.C.D., De Exemptione Regularium, X-188 pp., 1921.
13. Schaaf, Rev. Valentine Theodore, O.F.M., S.T.B., J.C.D., The Cloister, X-180 pp., 1921.
14. Burke, Rev. Thomas Joseph, S.T.D., J.C.D., Competence in Ecclesiastical Tribunals, IV-117 pp., 1922.
15. Leech, Rev. George Leo, J.C.D., A Comparative Study of the Constitution "Apostolicae Sedis" and the "Codex Juris Canonici," 179 pp., 1922.
16. Motry, Rev. Hubert Louis, S.T.D., J.C.D., Diocesan Faculties According to the Code of Canon Law, II-167 pp., 1922.
17. Murphy, Rev. George Lawrence, J.C.D., Delinquencies and Penalties in The Administration and the Reception of the Sacraments, IV-121 pp., 1923.
18. O'Reilly, Rev. John Anthony, S.T.B., J.C.D., Ecclesiastical Sepulture in the New Code of Canon Law, II-129 pp., 1923.
19. Michalicka, Rev. Wenceslas Cyrill, O.S.B., J.C.D., Judicial Procedure in Dismissal of Clerical Exempt Religious, 107 pp., 1923.
20. Dargin, Rev. Edward Vincent, S.T.B., J.C.D., Reserved Cases According to the Code of Canon Law, IV-103 pp., 1924.

21. Godfrey, Rev. John A., S.T.B., J.C.D., The Right of Patronage According to the Code of Canon Law, 153 pp., 1924.
22. Hagedorn, Rev. Francis Edward, J.C.D., General Legislation on Indulgences, II-154 pp., 1924.
23. King, Rev. James Ignatius, J.C.D., The Administration of the Sacraments to Dying Non-Catholics, V-141 pp., 1924.
24. Winslow, Rev. Francis Joseph, O.F.M., J.C.D., Vicars and Prefects Apostolic, IV-149 pp., 1924.
25. Correa, Rev. Jose Servelion, S.T.L., J.C.D., La Potestad Legislativa de la Iglesia Catolica, IV-127 pp., 1925.
26. Dugan, Rev. Henry Francis, A.M., J.C.D., The Judiciary Department of the Diocesan Curia, 87 pp., 1925.
27. Keller, Rev. Charles Frederick, S.T.B., J.C.D., Mass Stipends, 167 pp., 1925.
28. Paschang, Rev. John Linus, J.C.D., The Sacramentals According to the Code of Canon Law, 129 pp., 1925.
29. Pointek, Rev. Cyrillus, O.F.M., S.T.B., J.C.D., De Indulto Exclaustrationis necnon Saecularizationis, XIII-289 pp., 1925.
30. Kearney, Rev. Richard Joseph, S.T.B., J.C.D., Sponsors at Baptism According to the Code of Canon Law, IV-127 pp., 1925.
31. Bartlett, Rev. Chester Joseph, A.M., LL.B., J.C.D., The Tenure of Parochial Property in the United States of America, V-108 pp., 1926.
32. Kilker, Rev. Adrian Jerome, J.C.D., Extreme Unction, V-425 pp., 1926.
33. McCormick, Rev. Robert Emmett, J.C.D., Confessors of Religious, VIII-266 pp., 1926.
34. Miller, Rev. Newton Thomas, J.C.D., Founded Masses According to the Code of Canon Law, VII-93 pp., 1926.
35. Roelker, Rev. Edward G., S.T.D., J.C.D., Principles of Privilege According to the Code of Canon Law, XI-166 pp., 1926.
36. Bakalarczyk, Rev. Richardus, M.I.C., J.U.D., De Novitiatu, VIII-208 pp., 1927.
37. Pizzuti, Rev. Lawrence, O.F.M., J.U.L., De Parochis Religiosis, 1927. (Not Printed.)
38. Bliley, Rev. Nicholas Martin, O.S.B., J.C.D., Altars According to the Code of Canon Law, XIX-132 pp., 1927.
39. Brown, Mr. Brendan Francis, A.B., LL.M., J.U.D., The Canonical Juristic Personality with Special Reference to its Status in the United States of America, V-212 pp., 1927.
40. Cavanaugh, Rev. William Thomas, C.P., J.U.D., The Reservation of the Blessed Sacrament, VIII-101 pp., 1927.
41. Doheny, Rev. William J., C.S.C., A.B., J.U.D., Church Property: Modes of Acquisition, X-118 pp., 1927.
42. Feldhaus, Rev. Aloysius H., C.PP.S., J.C.D., Oratories, IX-141 pp., 1927.
43. Kelly, Rev. James Patrick, A.B., J.C.D., The Jurisdiction of the Simple Confessor, X-208 pp., 1927.

44. NEUBERGER, REV. NICHOLAS J., J.C.D., Canon 6 or the Relation of the Codex Juris Canonici to the Preceding Legislation, V-95 pp. 1927.
45. O'KEEFE, REV. GERALD MICHAEL, J.C.D., Matrimonial Dispensations, Powers of Bishops, Priests, and Confessors, VIII-232 pp., 1927.
46. QUIGLEY, REV. JOSEPH A. M., A.B., J.C.D., Condemned Societies, 139 pp., 1927.
47. ZAPLOTNIK, REV. JOHANNES LEO, J.C.D., De Vicariis Foraneis, X-142 pp., 1927.
48. DUSKIE, REV. JOHN ALOYSIUS, A.B., J.C.D., The Canonical Status of the Orientals in the United States, VIII-196 pp., 1928.
49. HYLAND, REV. FRANCIS EDWARD, J.C.D., Excommunication, Its Nature, Historical Development and Effects, VIII-181 pp., 1928.
50. REINMANN, REV. GERALD JOSEPH, O.M.C., J.C.D., The Third Order Secular of Saint Francis, 201 pp., 1928.
51. SCHENK, REV. FRANCIS J., J.C.D., The Matrimonial Impediments of Mixed Religion and Disparity of Cult, XVI-318 pp., 1929.
52. COADY, REV. JOHN JOSEPH, S.T.D., J.U.D., A.M., The Appointment of Pastors, VIII-150 pp., 1929.
53. KAY, REV. THOMAS HENRY, J.C.D., Competence in Matrimonial Procedure, VIII-164 pp., 1929.
54. TURNER, REV. SIDNEY JOSEPH, C.P., J.U.D., The Vow of Poverty, XLIX-217 pp., 1929.
55. KEARNEY, REV. RAYMOND A., A.B., S.T.D., J.C.D., The Principles of Delegation, VII-149 pp., 1929.
56. CONRAN, REV. EDWARD JAMES, A.B., J.C.D., The Interdict, V-163 pp., 1930.
57. O'NEIL, REV. WILLIAM H., J.C.D., Papal Rescripts of Favor, VII-218 pp., 1930.
58. BASTNAGEL, REV. CLEMENT VINCENT, J.U.D., The Appointment of Parochial Adjutants and Assistants, XV-257 pp., 1930.
59. FERRY, REV. WILLIAM A., A.B., J.C.D., Stole Fees, V-136, pp., 1930.
60. COSTELLO, REV. JOHN MICHAEL, A.B., J.C.D., Domicile and Quasi-Domicile, VII-201 pp., 1930.
61. KREMER, REV. MICHAEL NICHOLAS, A.B., S.T.B., J.C.D., Church Support in the United States, VI-136 pp., 1930.
62. ANGULO, REV. LUIS, C.M., J.C.D., Legislation de la Iglesia sobre la intencion en la application de la Santa Misa, VII-104 pp., 1931.
63. FREY, REV. WOLFGANG, NORBERT, O.S.B., A.B., J.C.D., The Act of Religious Profession, VIII-174 pp., 1931.
64. ROBERTS, REV. JAMES BRENDAN, A.B., J.C.D., The Banns of Marriage, XIV-140 pp., 1931.
65. RYDER, REV. RAYMOND ALOYSIUS, A.B., J.C.D., Simony, IX-151 pp., 1931.
66. CAMPAGNA, REV. ANGELO, PH.D., J.U.D., Il Vicario Generale del Vescovo, VII-205 pp., 1931.

67. Cox, Rev. Joseph Godfrey, A.B., J.C.D., The Administration of Seminaries, VI-124 pp., 1931.
68. Gregory, Rev. Donald J., J.U.D., The Pauline Privilege, XV-165 pp., 1931.
69. Donohue, Rev. John F., J.C.D., The Impediment of Crime, VII-110 pp., 1931.
70. Dooley, Rev. Eugene A., O.M.I., J.C.D., Church Law on Sacred Relics, IX-143 pp., 1931.
71. Orth, Rev. Clement Raymond, O.M.C., J.C.D., The Approbation of Religious Institutes, 171 pp., 1931.
72. Pernicone, Rev. Joseph M., A.B., J.C.D., The Ecclesiastical Prohibition of Books, XII-267 pp., 1932.
73. Clinton, Rev. Connell, A.B., J.C.D., The Paschal Precept, IX-108 pp., 1932.
74. Donnelly, Rev. Francis B., A.M., S.T.L., J.C.D., The Diocesan Synod, VIII-125 pp., 1932.
75. Torrente, Rev. Camilo, C.M.F., J.C.D., Las Processiones Sagradas, V-145 pp., 1932.
76. Murphy, Rev. Edwin J., C.PP.S., J.C.D., Suspension Ex Informata Conscientia, XI-122 pp., 1932.
77. Mackenzie, Rev. Eric F., A.M., S.T.L., J.C.D., The Delict of Heresy in its Commission, Penalization, Absolution, VII-124 pp., 1932.
78. Lyons, Rev. Avitus E., S.T.B., J.C.D., The Collegiate Tribunal of First Instance, XI-147 pp., 1932.
79. Connolly, Rev. Thomas A., J.C.D., Appeals, XI-195, pp., 1932.
80. Sangmeister, Rev. Joseph V., A.B., J.C.D., Force and Fear as Precluding Matrimonial Consent, V-211, pp., 1932.
81. Jaeger, Rev. Leo A., A.B., J.C.D., The Administration of Vacant and Quasi-Vacant Episcopal Sees in the United States, IX-229 pp., 1932.
82. Rimlinger, Rev. Herbert T., J.C.D., Error Invalidating Matrimonial Consent, VII-79 pp., 1932.
83. Barrett, Rev. John D. M., S.S., J.C.D., A Comparative Study of the Third Plenary Council of Baltimore and the Code, IX-221 pp., 1932.
84. Carberry, Rev. John J., Ph.D., S.T.D., J.C.D., The Juridical Form of Marriage, X-177 pp., 1934.
85. Dolan, Rev. John L., A.B., J.C.D., The Defensor Vinculi, XII, 157 pp., 1934.
86. Hannan, Rev. Jerome D., A.M., S.T.D., LL.B., J.C.D., The Canon Law of Wills, IX-517 pp., 1934.
87. Lemieux, Rev. Delisle A., A.M., J.C.D., The Sentence in Ecclesiastical Procedure, IX-131 pp., 1934.
88. O'Rourke, Rev. James J., A.B., J.C.D., Parish Registers, VII-109 pp., 1934.
89. Timlin, Rev. Bartholomew, O.F.M., A.M., J.C.D., Conditional Matrimonial Consent, X-381 pp., 1934.

90. Wahl, Rev. Francis X., A.B., J.C.D., The Matrimonial Impediments of Consanguinity and Affinity, VI-125 pp., 1934.
91. White, Rev. Robert J., A.B., LL.B., S.T.B., J.C.D., Canonical Ante-Nuptial Promises and the Civil Law, VI-152 pp., 1934.
92. Herrera, Rev. Antonio Parra, O.C.D., J.C.D., Legislacion Ecclesiastica sobra el Ayuno y la Abstinencia, XI-191 pp., 1935.
93. Kennedy, Rev. Edwin J., J.C.D., The Special Matrimonial Process in Cases of Evident Nullity, X-165 pp., 1935.
94. Manning, Rev. John J., A.B., J.C.D., Presumption of Law in Matrimonial Procedure, XI-111 pp., 1935.
95. Moeder, Rev. John M., J.C.D., The Proper Bishop for Ordination and Dimissorial Letters, VII-135 pp., 1935.
96. O'Mara, Rev. William A., A.B., J.C.D., Canonical Causes for Matrimonial Dispensations, IX-155 pp., 1935.
97. Reilly, Rev. Peter, J.C.D., Residence of Pastors, IX-81 pp., 1935.
98. Smith, Rev. Mariner T., O.P., S.T.Lr., J.C.D., The Penal Law for Religious, VII-169 pp., 1935.
99. Whalen, Rev. Donald W., A.M., J.C.D., The Value of Testimonial Evidence in Matrimonial Procedure, XIII-297 pp., 1935.
100. Cleary, Rev. Joseph F., J.C.D., Canonical Limitations on the Alienation of Church Property, VIII-141 pp., 1936.
101. Glynn, Rev. John C., J.C.D., The Promoter of Justice, XX-337 pp., 1936.
102. Brennan, Rev. James H., S.S., M.A., S.T.B., J.C.L., The Simple Convalidation of Marriage.
103. Brunini, Rev. Joseph Bernard, J.C.L., The Clerical Obligations of Canons 139 and 142.
104. Connor, Rev. Maurice, A.B., J.C.L., The Administrative Removal of Pastors.
105. Guilfoyle, Rev. Merlin Joseph, J.C.L., Custom.
106. Hughes, Rev. James Austin, A.B., A.M., J.C.L., Witnesses in Criminal Trials of Clerics.
107. Jansen, Rev. Raymond J., A.B., S.T.L., J.C.L., Canonical Provisions for Catechetical Instruction.
108. Kealy, Rev. John James, A.B., J.C.L., The Introductory Libellus in Church Court Procedure.
109. McManus, Rev. James Edward, C.SS.R., J.C.L., The Administration of Temporal Goods in Religious Institutes.
110. Moriarty, Rev. Eugene James, J.C.L., Oaths in Ecclesiastical Courts.
111. Rainer, Rev. Eligius George, C.SS.R., J.C.L., Suspension of Clerics.
112. Reilly, Rev. Thomas F., C.SS.R., J.C.L., Visitation of Religious.

www.ingramcontent.com/pod-product-compliance
Lightning Source LLC
LaVergne TN
LVHW050205080826
844660LV00012B/361

* 9 7 8 0 8 1 3 2 2 2 9 2 9 *